COACHING THE ZONE
AND
MAN-TO-MAN PRESSING DEFENSES

COACHING THE ZONE

AND

MAN-TO-MAN PRESSING DEFENSES

Neal Baisi

Head Basketball Coach
West Virginia
Institute of Technology

Englewood Cliffs, N.J.

Prentice-Hall, Inc.

PRINTED IN THE UNITED STATES OF AMERICA

13939—MO

ACKNOWLEDGMENTS

Grateful appreciation is herewith expressed to all persons who have shared in the preparation of this book. Particularly helpful has been the assistance of Goodrich "Pete" Phillips, my assistant coach, who has spent many hours of hard work presenting valuable contributions.

For my incentive, I acknowledge my college president, Dr. William B. Axtell. It was his suggestion to faculty members that they attempt more publications that inspired me to make this effort.

The author is also grateful for the assistance of Dr. C. W. Stallard, Jr., a physician in the Montgomery area and a friend the athletes here at Tech will never forget.

I wish to give special thanks to Sidney Maynard for the illustrations and Catherine Roberts and Frances Shrewsbury for the typing.

PREFACE

In keeping with the rapid change of basketball, this guide for pressing defenses represents a thorough study of the future of basketball defenses.

In preparing this book about the great game of basketball, we do so with the hope that you, the reader, will find something that will prove interesting and profitable.

In this book, I have tried to point out the importance of the press to you so your team will be ready for the situation, whether ahead or behind. If your team is beaten by a better team without a surprise attack or without the other team having better knowledge of the game, then you can hold your head high even in defeat.

CONTENTS

12 CONTENTS

1

WHY THE PRESS?

During the relatively short time since Dr. Naismith nailed up his two peach baskets at Springfield College and drafted the original thirteen rules for the game of basketball, there have been few major changes in the game, especially in the area of defense. This book describes one of these major contributions.

THE MODERN GAME

Since basketball has not experienced many contemporary changes in its offense, defense, and basic strategy, it perhaps has not kept pace with the other factors of the game. Basketball in its comparatively short life has become highly organized; from "biddy" basketball to the professional ranks. Consequently, basketball players, at the different levels of organization, operate on a much higher skill level than the earlier players. The participants, then, have been and presumably still are improving. Yet they are still participating in many instances against defenses that have not basically changed. This is reflected in the increased scoring of modern basketball.

The shooting of modern basketball teams is becoming so

13

effective that one must press, at times, in order to hinder their shooting by keeping them constantly off-balance. Also, the intricate screening plays and patterns that are now being employed more and more, are getting the offensive team the good shot. This is true only when a team has time to set up its offense. The pressing defenses are designed to prevent this. Properly employed it tends to disorganize the opposition, especially the play-making guards.

It is my belief that practicing and playing pressing defenses more thoroughly develops basketball ability in the individual player than any other method known.

A college player who uses man-to-man defenses and the zone pressing defenses is a more versatile player than one who plays the different types of slow, drop-back defenses. The former has a much better chance to develop more skill in more different areas.

Requirements for Pressing

These types of defenses also make room for many boys who could not otherwise participate under other systems of play. This is true because the prerequisites for playing zone press and man-to-man press are not all physical ones. Pressing defenses demand dedication, desire, and a deep sense of responsibility. The physical skills are subordinated by the preceding psychological characteristics which are so necessary. If the psychological characteristics are present, the physical skills will develop quickly.

You are probably saying to yourself by now that you feel the above to be true in your system also. Yes, all systems demand all of these characteristics to a degree. The pressing defenses, the way we play them, demand all of these characteristics to a degree much more pronounced than one will find on the average team.

Pressing defenses demand the highest degree of cooperation. This system tends to create order and endows the players with the utmost confidence in it. This is attributed to the fact that this pressing system requires each player to know the exact whereabouts of each other player and, in addition, carry out a designated assignment. In many instances a player has to reach beyond his limits, or at least what he thinks are his limits. The concept of "the difficult takes time; the impossible, a little longer," will be discussed later in the book.

Advantages of the Presses

One of the advantages of the zone press and the man-to-man pressing defenses is its potential economic value. The zone press, especially, is a tremendous crowd-pleaser. If operated correctly it cannot help but catch the fancy of the spectators. When I began to develop and to employ the zone press, the attendance at our games rose almost as much as the team scoring (100-plus points per game). This brought our school, town, and state copious amounts of state and national publicity.

The colorful aspect of the pressing defenses has injected a tremendous amount of pride and spirit into our student body. During games when the presses are suddenly brought into play they are met with great gusto.

When you employ the pressing defenses constantly, your opponents fully expect to be pressed and consequently they have to prepare for it. However, many times it requires more time to come up with counter-strategies than it does to install the pressing defenses themselves. Also, when the teams reach the point of expecting the pressing defenses, you may choose to use something else to throw them off stride.

These defenses are especially devastating to the teams that use a semi-control ball type of play. These teams usually have elaborate plays and patterns which are very ineffective against the zone presses. One of the reasons for this is that most of these presses resemble both a zone defense and a man-to-man defense. Actually, they are parts of both. This situation usually creates offensive confusion, since the offensive team has difficulty in deciding whether to use a zone or man-to-man offense. It is usually too late by this time to efficiently set up a new offense.

Our many pressing defenses have so many similarities to each other that scouting by the opponent is very difficult. We have had scouts tell us that we used a certain defense in the first period when we had actually used five different defenses.

Even though all of these positive features more than sufficiently justify the zone press and the man-to-man press defenses, there is yet one more feature. It is more logical and reasonable than all of the preceding. Paradoxically, this most significant point has been left until last with the hope that it will be the most impressionable.

Why the press? When your team is behind in a game, sooner or later, you will be forced to press in order to obtain possession of the ball. An ordinary "man-on-man" press is not sufficient for this purpose, especially against a team that is well organized.

On the other hand, if your team is winning you should be very familiar with the different presses because the opposition will be forced to press you for the ball. If you are not prepared to combat the pressing defenses, the result could be tragic and chaotic.

Zone and man-to-man presses will undoubtedly make a significant contribution to the game of basketball.

2

INDIVIDUAL DEFENSE

"The difficult takes time; the impossible, a little longer."
This, in short, summarizes our theory of individual defense.

From the time each player begins as a freshman with the team, he is indoctrinated by this philosophy. Many of the defenses to be discussed are unique and different and almost all require very difficult assignments under certain situations. Each boy assumes that he has certain limits to his ability. Usually, this assumed limit is not sufficient to carry out his defensive assignment. However, unless he is shown differently, he may not exceed his assumed limit of ability.

As in a boy's academic work, he has untold ability that will perhaps never be uncovered. It is a familiar story of two students with nearly identical intelligent quotients but one student doing much better than the other. This is also true of athletic ability. It is impossible to point out one specific thing and present it as the reason for one student doing better than another with equal ability. It can be said that one had greater motivation than the other. Motivation then is the key in raising a player's skill level.

While this process of showing a boy that he can do much

more than he previously supposed he could takes place, self-confidence is developing in the player and is replacing uncertainty and doubt. It is of the utmost importance to have players that believe in themselves and in what they are doing. If one player lacks self-confidence, it is quickly sensed by the other players and they, in turn, lose confidence in him also.

After being exposed to this type of thinking for a year, our younger players do not question, in their minds, whether or not a certain thing is beyond their ability. Many find, to their amazement, that there are many difficult tasks that they can perform, with practice, that previously they had deemed beyond their ability.

THE PLAYER—HIS ATTITUDE

The player's attitude is the most important single factor in playing the man-to-man press and the zone press defenses.

His attitude must be one of complete dedication. We like boys who are quickly and easily challenged. You may count yourself among the fortunate if you happen to have that rare type personality on your team—the "hardnosed" basketball player. This type of boy is a true "one hundred per cent-er" and will give you every ounce of his strength. Every team should have at least one boy like this when the pressing defenses are constantly employed. This particular type player is an emotional one and under the stimulus of stress, he operates very efficiently on adrenalin energy. He is very dependable because his motivation runs deep and is usually very meaningful to him.

The relationship of a player to his fellow player is a

most important one. It must be one of "togetherness."
There is absolutely no place on an athletic team for a boy
who does not get along well with the other players, regardless of his ability. He will be a source of constant trouble
for you. The team morale may be weakened by him. The
most important criteria of the player-to-player relationship
is that they think together and feel that special kinship
that only athletics affords.

Conditioning and Training

Our conditioning and training program is a most rigid
one. In order to play our type of basketball for a full game
a player must be in the very peak of physical conditioning.
Our style of play is the most strenuous style known today.
We must be as effective in the last period as we are in the
first.

A 100 per cent effort is expected in any move that is
made. It is the coach's responsibility to see that this can
be done. You can do this by your 2 or 2½ hour practice
sessions being well organized with conditioning in mind.
After the initial conditioning, run the team through an individual drill for 15 minutes and explain that this is 5 minutes longer than the first period.

I feel a player is not tired until he falls to the floor
without the strength to catch himself with his hands. I tell
my boys that you are tired when you fall on your face and
do not have the strength to pull yourself up. Just because
there is no feeling left, you are not necessarily exhausted,
if you are a real competitor. Keep going and you will catch
your wind. Learn to play without feeling. Then you are a
real basketball player. If you are to build a winning team,
hard work is necessary on the part of coach and player.

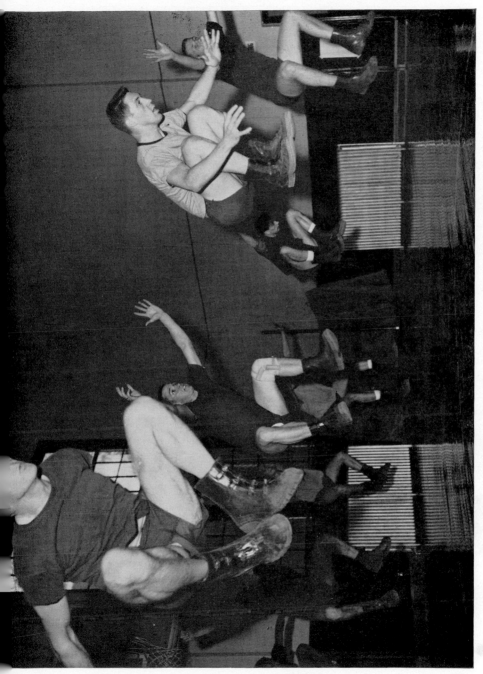

PLATE 1. *A Jumping Drill Designed to Condition and Strengthen the Legs.* (Note the galoshes for added weight.)

PLATE 2. *Another Conditioning Drill, the Boxer Shuffle.* (Galoshes make this a strenuous drill.)

Good training is absolutely vital to the success of the team. Use of alcohol, smoking, staying out late, and any undesirable habit, can only be a hindrance to a team. We make it very clear to our boys that anyone caught drinking is automatically removed from the team. A boy cannot drink and still play our 100 per cent basketball. Smoking is penalized by expulsion from the squad for all upperclassmen. Naturally some freshmen smoked in high school. The first time a freshman is caught smoking, we run him six miles. If he makes the six miles, he may remain on the team. The next offense brings immediate expulsion.

In everything we do we like to be the very best. When we stay at hotels, we have a room check before we leave to make sure that everything is just as we found it. We do not allow cursing at anytime and it is punishable at the rate of 25 laps per profane word. All of these things, we feel, instill individual and team pride in the boys. We point out that only the strong are able to play for us. Not only strength on the floor, but off the floor as well, is demanded.

DEFENSIVE FUNDAMENTALS

The role of fundamentals is a very vital one. The ability of your players to master fundamentals will determine whether you have an average or successful season. There is not one champion of any type today who has not mastered the fundamentals that are relative to his own area.

The practice of fundamentals is time-consuming, trying, and tedious, hard work. They can be mastered only by trial and error. It is imperative that they be done over and over so that they become automatic.

The following list of fundamentals are those that are

considered important in teaching the man-to-man press and the zone press.

1. Develop peripheral vision so that you may watch the ball and opponent at the same time.

2. Never trail your man. The minimum effort should put the defensive man at the side of the offensive player.

3. The knees should always be bent, ready to spring and move. One foot should be in front of the other, and one arm should be up when your man has the ball in scoring areas.

4. Use the boxer shuffle and never cross your feet.

5. Do not switch unless it is absolutely necessary. Fight your way through screens.

6. If you must switch, the man that is closest to the basket is responsible for the call. Call either "Switch" or "Hold" only. Stay with the new man until you can switch back. Try to keep the man who was originally assigned to you.

7. Block out when the shot is taken. Stay between your man and the basket so that he cannot rebound. You are on defense until you get possession of the ball.

8. Give your man room when he doesn't have the ball and is on the outside. When the ball is on the opposite side of the floor, give your man room and sag toward the middle. Never lose sight of your man, regardless of the position of the ball.

9. When you have given your man space and he receives a pass, do not rush headlong. Move quickly and check him so that he does not drive.

10. If a shot is faked, keep the right arm straight. If you leave your feet on a faked shot, come down with the arm still extended. This way you are still prepared to defend against the shot. Never bother a shooter with sweeping motion of the arm, because as it goes down, he will be able to shoot over you, and it leads to fouls.

11. Do not foul. A good defensive man who maintains his correct position and keeps working does not need

to foul. A poor guard fouls often because his man gets ahead of him. It many times indicates that a player is loafing.

12. Defense is about 80 per cent determination. Almost anyone can guard well if he works at it. Hound your man unmercifully until he knows who is toughest.

13. Talk to each other on defense, especially on shifts.

14. Do not go so far and then fall off your opponent. Go all the way through the defense with him.

15. If your man has the ball, keep one arm extended full height to block his vision of the basket; the other arm should be carried low for use in stealing the ball.

16. The calling of "Switch" is the responsibility of the player guarding the man who sets up the screen.

17. Learn all of your opponents' tricks. Never let them score on the same maneuver twice.

18. Be prepared to switch to help your teammate when it is necessary. Talk to him to let him know who your man is.

19. The defensive man who allows his man too much freedom will be replaced. Each man must contain his opponent to remain in the ball game.

20. When your man has the ball and has not used his dribble, watch his middle section. It cannot fake you.

21. In guarding the dribbler, get the rhythm of the dribble up and down with the hand in time with the ball. The steal should be made on the downward flight of the ball, with the same downward motion of the hand, to prevent fouling. Never reach in or slap at the ball.

22. If you have a jump ball with an opponent other than your man, be sure to point out your opponent to the teammate who guards the man with whom you are jumping.

23. Never enter a game without thorough knowledge of each player's strong and weak points.

24. Loose balls should be tackled on the floor.

25. Contest all passes to your opponent when he is in scoring territory.

26. If double cutting off of the pivot, allow room for your teammate to slide through and switch on the second man cutting.

27. Be sure to keep defensive balance at all times. Always have at least one man back toward midcourt as a safety man to stop the fast break.

28. Play in front of all pivot men until they get as far out as the foul line.

29. Step back one step to let your teammate slide through if your man is not too close to the basket or if your man does not have the ball, and then close in again.

30. When a guard is driven into the post, he should aim for the inside shoulder of the post man so that he can roll to the inside of the new man on the switch.

31. Slide when the play is outside, but switch when screens occur near the basket.

32. When guarding the man out-of-bounds, concentrate on the ball alone and not the man.

33. When playing a zone defense, make the man with the ball do something. Force him into passing or moving. While he is moving, the defense has time to adjust. Always move him toward the middle if he is on the end line. When the ball handler dribbles down the sideline, do not let him inside. Drive him to the end line and then inside.

34. Do not allow three-point plays. They are very demoralizing.

3

SCOUTING AND MEASUREMENT

With as many as fifteen or twenty different defenses in our repertoire, we have to have some means of evaluating the opposing team in order to know what defenses may be used to the best advantage. We like to scout every team on our schedule but this is usually not possible.

When you establish a reputation as a "fast break and pressing" team, it is imperative that you know something about the other team. Scouting not only provides information on the opposing team, but on your own team as well, if you so desire. We are constantly searching for new ways to evaluate our own performances. We do this by charting each boy on the team in all areas. Each boy has a rating for each game which is calculated from charts that are kept on him. According to the number of units he receives for a game, he is assigned a rank number from one to ten.

Good scouting provides a great deal of information. Your own team will benefit from the specific facts of such a report and they will benefit mentally. It gives a comfortable and secure feeling in knowing exactly what to expect.

There is nothing so disturbing to a team than to realize that they do not know what is going on. Good scouting can almost eliminate the crushing element of surprise.

Individual Scouting

Our defensive system is set up to take every possible advantage of a team's weaknesses. Several of our defenses could not operate successfully if the other team did not have a weak player. It is this player that you must find in your scouting. His weakness may be ever so small, but not so small that it cannot be put to some good use.

This individual that we look for may not, necessarily, be weak from the standpoint of skill or motor ability. His may be an emotional or personality weakness. This type of defect is much more detrimental to him than any motor defect could be. Many times this "weak" player may be the best player on the team.

Several years ago we were meeting a rival in a game in which we were the underdog. This was due to the fact that the opposing team had a great guard. He had a very high average and was very adept at every phase of the game. In scouting this team several times before we met, we suddenly realized that this player brought the ball up the court by himself, and took great pride in it. Several times we observed him when he would wave a teammate back down the floor who had come to give him a hand. This was an insult to this boy. It all but told everyone that he could not bring it up by himself. He was very cocky about this one aspect of the game. Egomania was his downfall.

We set up a special "trap" defense in the back court. Our guards led him to a certain spot on the floor and then double teamed him. They stole the ball from him time and again, and when they did not steal it, they got a jump ball. He was completely shattered after the first ten minutes of play and literally gave up. The coach took him out of the game and he did not return that night.

At any time he could have avoided this trap by passing off to his fellow guard and working the ball slowly up the floor. Due to this peculiar obsession to bring the ball down by himself, he destroyed himself and his team along with him.

The individual characteristics that we are concerned with are as follows:

1. Height
2. Weight
3. Is he a team player?
4. Does he have a strong competitive spirit?
5. How does he rebound?
6. How does he shoot?
7. How fast is he?
8. Is he in good condition?
9. Is he an ambidextrous dribbler? Shooter?
10. Which side does he favor?
11. Does he dribble high?
12. Is he a good ball handler?
13. Does he try to draw fouls?
14. How well does he shoot fouls?
15. What things seem to "rattle" him?
16. Does he attempt to tip in missed shots?
17. Does he get back on defense quickly?
18. Is he easily faked out of position?
19. Does he take chances on defense?
20. Is he a good defensive player?

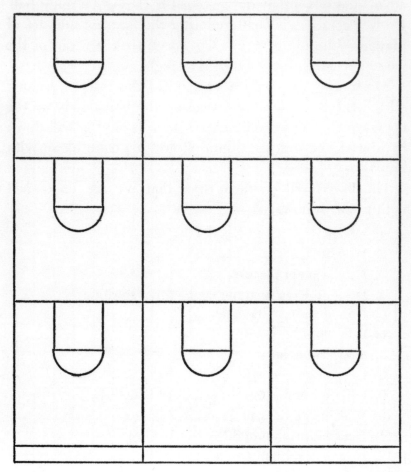

FIGURE 1. *Shot Chart.* Shot Code: 1. Set Shot   4. (Fast break)
                                      2. Jump Shot   lay up
                                      3. Lay up   5. Hook
                                                      6. Tap

TEAM: ———————— DATE: ————————

| No. | NAME | SHOTS | | | REBOUNDS | | | LOSS OF BALL | | | | Assists | Inter-ception | Blocked Shot |
		Attempts	Total Made	Total	Offensive	Defensive	Total	Bad Pass	Travel	3 Secs.	Other			
	TEAM TOTALS													

FIGURE 2. Statistical Chart.

We chart each player's shooting on both our team and the opponent's team. Each shot taken in the game is recorded by: 1. type of shot; 2. made or missed; 3. its location on the court. Figure 1 illustrates the type of shot chart that we use, and its code.

This chart tells us where most of the opposing team's shots originated. This, in turn, shows us where we must bolster our defense. If too many close-in shots or tap-ins appear on the chart, it points the finger at the man who is supposed to be defensing the area around the basket. By showing the type of shot that is taken by each player, it reveals the type of shot that we must not allow them to shoot. It is my experience that most real good shooters lose some of their effectiveness if they are forced to shoot several feet farther away from the basket than they like. We plan our defense according to where the good shooter likes to shoot.

Besides this information, we keep all of the statistical data on both teams such as fouls, shots, rebounds, and turnovers. Our statistical chart is shown in Figure 2.

We collect all of this data on our own team and break it down into percentages. It is then transferred to a cumulative graph that runs for an entire season. In Figure 3 you will find an example of a graph showing an individual player's shooting percentage for each game throughout the season. These graphs stimulate a lot of interest on the part of our players. Each player's graphs are kept on a large bulletin board in the dressing room and the players can be seen grouped around them the day following a game. It represents a challenge to each player and it makes them work harder to improve.

Of course, the player with a very low mark, is joshed

and kidded in the spirit of fun by the other players and this tends to create team spirit and good player relationships.

An area of scouting that is of prime importance to us is the area that will affect our defensive presses. Look for the formations that they use to bring the ball up the floor against the press. Chart these formations with each player that is used in them. It is just as valuable to know the individual players as it is to know the formation or pattern.

Attempt to record all plays used in bringing up the ball, especially screening plays. It is imperative that you have an idea on these points so that you may prepare your defenses. Many back court plays and formations may be stymied by the selection and use of the proper defense.

SELF-EVALUATION

It is important to obtain the opinions of the players themselves as to the stature of their performances. It is important for everyone to have the ability to scrutinize themselves, as they are, and to constructively criticize.

There are two types of evaluation that we use from time to time. These are objective and subjective evaluations or measures.

For an objective measure we use a rating scale. Each boy, after the game, receives a rating scale and he rates himself in different areas as he feels he should be rated. The ratings are graded *excellent, good, fair* and *poor.* At different times, each boy on the team will rate four other boys on a night's performance. This gives us more evaluations on each boy and tends to make the results more statistically valid. It is good to know what each boy thinks of the performances of the other players.

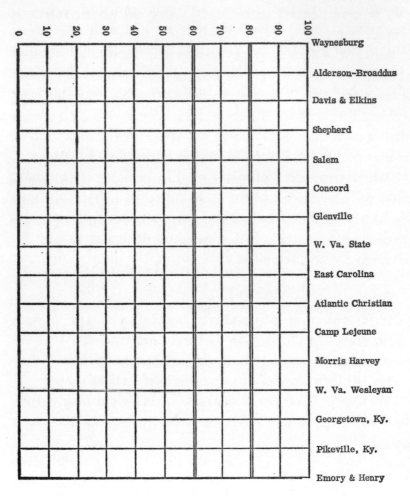

FIGURE 3. Graph on Player Shooting Percentage.

For a subjective measure of performance we use the "paragraph" method. After the game each boy writes, in paragraph form, everything that he did well and everything that he did not do well. This written evaluation should list each time that his man scored and the reason that it happened. It should further explain any turnovers that might have occurred.

Scouting and Evaluating the Fast Break

Since we are a fast breaking team and most of the teams that we play are also, it is essential to scout the opponent team. The following items are the things that we deem necessary to know in order to combat the fast break.

1. Know their middle man or the one that they depend upon most often to lead the break.
2. How many options do they have on the outlet pass?
3. Where do they like to throw the outlet pass?
4. How fast are their three break men?
5. Do they ever try to tip out to start the break?
6. Do they attempt to fast break after a foul shot?
7. Do they ever sneak a guard away for the long pass?
8. How well does the middle man shoot from the foul circle?
9. On the break, do they like to pass the ball around or does the middle man dribble it all the way to the foul circle.
10. Where do they like to shoot on the fast break?

After this knowledge has been accumulated you will have more than enough information upon which to base your defense.

In evaluating our own fast break, we chart each individual fast break that occurs in the game. This chart (Figure 4) indicates whether or not the fast break was successful and if it was not, it gives the reason why. Further breakdown of this information after the game and its correlation with the other data that we gather, gives us a very good picture of what has happened.

To round out our scouting report we always have a list of items that we look to rather closely in determining the general pattern of the team as a whole. They are as follows:

1. What kind of defense do they use?
2. Do they employ a full court press?
3. Do they rebound well?
4. Are they weak against screens?
5. Do they switch on defense?
6. Do they ever use a zone defense? What type?
7. How do they play their pivot man?
8. Do they get back quick on defense?
9. Do they try to tip out rebounds?
10. Do they block out and rebound well?
11. Do they use offensive patterns and plays or both?
12. How do they pass in to the pivot?
13. Do they drive a lot?
14. Do they "give and go"?
15. Do they ever play deliberate ball?
16. Are they a good ball handling team?
17. Do they have a good "second effort"?
18. Do they have any bench strength?
19. Do they appear to be in good physical condition?
20. How do they set up on jump balls?

BP-Bad Pass (Type & why)   J-Jump Ball (Tap where)   OB-Out of Bounds
W-Walking   MS-Missed Shot (Type & reason)   F-Foul (Type)
DO-Double Dribble   S-3 Second rule   BS-Blocked Shot (Type)
    SB-Stolen Ball

| | WEST VIRGINIA TECH | | | | | | | OPPONENTS | | | | | | |
| | FAST BREAK | | | SET OFFENSE | | | | FAST BREAK | | | SET OFFENSE | | |
	Made	Foul	Loss	Made	Foul	Loss		Made	Foul	Loss	Made	Foul	Loss
1							1						
2							2						
3							3						
4							4						
5							5						
6							6						
7							7						
8							8						
9							9						
10							10						
11							11						
12							12						
13							13						
14							14						
15							15						
16							16						
17							17						
18							18						
19							19						
20							20						
21							21						
22							22						
23							23						
24							24						
25							25						
26							26						
27							27						
28							28						
29							29						
30							30						
31							31						
32							32						
33							33						
34							34						
35							35						
36							36						
37							37						
38							38						
39							39						
40							40						
41							41						
42							42						
43							43						
44							44						
45							45						
46							46						
47							47						
48							48						

FIGURE 4. Fast Break Evaluation Chart.

4

THE MAN-TO-MAN PRESS

O f all the pressing defenses, the man-to-man press is the most basic. Most pressing defenses have sprung from the man-to-man defense. The myriad of different types of presses all use the man-to-man principle in one way or another.

There are four basic man-to-man defenses that we use. There are variations of each of these four. This offers several defenses that are similar, but that are different, in some manner, from each of the others.

FULL COURT

There are two separate variations of the full court press. We will call them 55A and 55B. 55A is the standard man-to-man press. Each man is assigned a man on the opponent team. It is his assignment to prevent his opponent from getting the ball, especially on the first pass. The main object is to harass the opposition to such an extent that they throw bad passes and commit other fundamental blunders that result in turnovers. Constant pressure must be kept on the offensive men. They should not be allowed to rest or even breathe easily as long as the full court press is being

used. This is the life blood of your press. If you have personnel who do not feel a special pride in the man-to-man
press and are not challenged by the difficulty of its assignments, you will have very little success with this type of
defensive system.

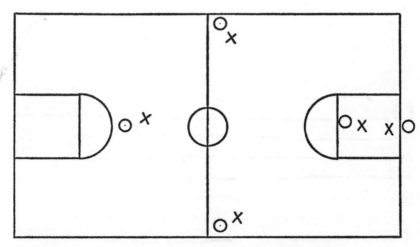

FIGURE 5. Basic Formation for 55A Press.

In Figure 5, the basic formation for 55A pressing defense
is given. Notice that the defensive players are overplaying
their men toward the ball. The crucial point of this press,
as in many of the presses, is the very first pass. You must
play for the first pass. Naturally, if you do not intercept the
first pass, the guards will have to play more cautiously.
They will not be able to overplay their men nearly as much
after the completion of the first pass.

The man who guards the man throwing the ball in from
out of bounds plays a key role in this press. First, he should
be one of your slower men, probably, the slower of the two
forwards. This takes a slow man out of the fast action
where speed is so necessary.

In guarding the man out of bounds, the ball must be the primary target. He should keep his arms waving in the man's face in order to disconcert him and to encourage the lob pass. At times, we will overguard the man out of bounds, to one side or another. This is to influence the man to pass to the side of the court that we want. Many times we want the first pass to go to the side where our fastest guard is playing. This increases the likelihood of an interception.

The player who takes the ball out of bounds for the opposing team, after we score, must be closely guarded to prevent him from getting off a quick pass. It is best to assign one man to immediately pick up the man out of bounds as soon as we score. This delaying action is designed, also, to let our center get down the floor in defensive position. We have one guard who drops back to mid-court to guard against the long pass, but, he releases as soon as the center gets back. This exchange must take place very quickly so that the guard can pick up his man in the back court. Impress on your center, or whoever is to drop back long, the importance of getting back as quickly as he possibly can in order to release the guard. The importance of delaying the pass in from the man out of bounds should now be clear.

The player who guards the man throwing the ball in bounds must be very alert after the pass has been made. Many times, after the pass-in, the passer will break very quickly past the guard and receive a return pass in the open.

It should be kept in mind that when any man manages to break in front of the defensive player, the defense has some quick, precise adjusting to do. First, the player who breaks in the open must be checked and contained by the

man closest to him. This will demand switching from his
own man to do this. Figure 6 illustrates how this is done.
Whenever a man breaks loose, each defensive man must
loosen up and drop toward the basket in order to cover.
Below are some basic rules to follow when a man breaks
loose:

1. The loose man should be picked up by the first possible defensive player.
2. All defensive men should drop toward the basket when
   a man breaks loose.
3. The player who picks up the loose man should attempt
   to control him and prevent him from advancing too
   quickly or throwing a good pass. Hands should be kept
   high to encourage a bounce pass which will give the
   defense more time to recover.
4. The defensive man who allows his opponent to get
   by him should retreat to the basket area with all possible haste and there pick up the first loose man.

This is the one situation that will occur with the most
frequency and that can cause the most damage to any man-
to-man defense. Of course, it is impossible to cover every
situation of this type in illustrations, especially in a game as
fluid as basketball. We always spend a great deal of time
in practice, setting up every possible situation that we can
of this type. We then point out the logical switches until
every man is perfectly clear on this phase. If an offensive
man manages to break away during a practice scrimmage
and is not properly contained, we immediately stop practice, set up the same situation, and correct it, being sure
that each man understands why. This is the most effective
and thorough way of teaching defenses of this type.

Our 55B defense is the second variation of the full court,
man-to-man press. It is used primarily against teams hav-

ing good guards that are difficult to press. One basic
thing that cannot be allowed against the man-to-man press
is the successful short pass. The offensive team must be
forced into throwing the long pass. This gives the defensive men more time in which to react and this results
in more interceptions. The shaded area in Figure 7 is

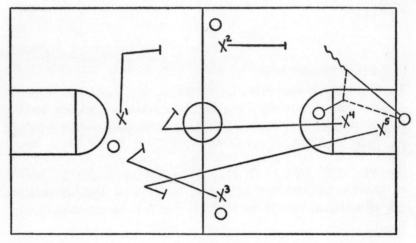

FIGURE 6. Adjusting 55A Press to a Loose Man.

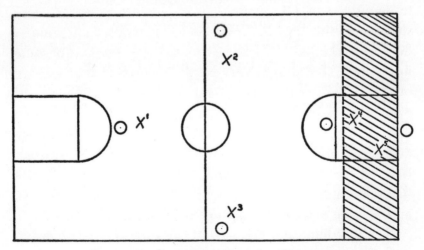

FIGURE 7. Basic Formation for 55B Press.

the area that must be protected against the first pass from out of bounds. In Figure 7, defensive player X^5, plays the shaded area instead of the man out of bounds. His assignment is to pick up any man who might break loose into the area or to double team an especially slippery guard. He may, also, double team a man on one side of the court in order to force the pass to the other side of the court. Most likely the man to whom we want them to pass is one who is weak fundamentally or who "cracks" under pressure of a pressing defense. We always try to take advantage of any man who has these weaknesses.

After the opposing team has successfully thrown in the ball, the defensive man who does not have a man picks up the player who passed the ball in from out of bounds. The defense must always be very alert after they have scored, in order to prevent the opposing team from quickly throwing the ball in short or throwing the long pass over our heads.

The Three-Quarter Court Press

We use the three-quarter court press only under special circumstances. Its main function is as an "observation press." Its basic formation is found in Figure 8.

Many times there are teams that we do not have an opportunity to scout. It is not known what type of formation they will use in order to bring the ball up the floor against the presses. We begin the game with the three-quarter press and do our scouting in the early part of the first period. We are interested in the following points:

1. How do they line up against the press?
2. What men go long?
3. What men go to the sides?

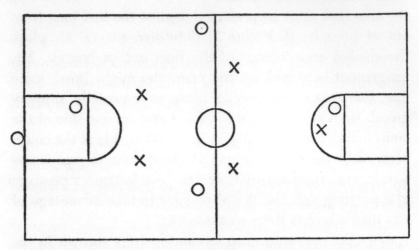

Figure 8. Basic Formation for the Three-Quarter Court Press.

4. Do they use back court screens?
5. Do they use a set pattern?
6. What guard do they depend on to bring up the ball?

After we find out these things, we select the pressing defenses which will best suit the situation.

Still another use of this defense is as a decoy defense. In this defense no one presses tight, intercepts any passes, or takes a chance whatsoever. We play it safe. We would deliberately appear to be inept at a pressing game. This tends to give the opposing team the idea that our team does not have a difficult press. It is important to instill, if possible, in the opponents a false sense of security. A sudden switch, to a very tight pressing defense, will, many times, completely fluster the opposing team and your tight press will be twice as effective as it usually is.

This defense will be of great strategic value to a coach and will improve the selection of proper defenses during the game.

The Half Court Press

The half court press operates on standard man-to-man principles. The only variation is the location on the court where the offense is picked up. This location is shown in Figure 9.

The opposing team is picked up very tightly on the mid-court line. From this point on, each player's assignment is to stop his man. This is one of the man-to-man defenses where we allow switching of men.

Many teams use elaborate systems of plays, many of which originate around the mid-court line. The signals for certain plays are transmitted by the guards to the other players. This is done in many ways. Some of these signals are as follows:

1. Raising the ball over the head.
2. Using finger signals, such as raising one, two, or three fingers.
3. Bouncing the ball in a certain manner.
4. Calling out play numbers.
5. By moving to a certain area on the floor.

If the guards are pressed very tightly, they should be worrying about how they are going to hang onto the ball instead of setting up plays. Our main objective is to stop the play signals. If a player has time to set up all of these plays, then our guards are not doing a half-way decent job of defense.

The Drop Back Man-to-Man Press

The drop back man-to-man defense combines both zone and man-to-man principles. It may be used as a primary or secondary defense. It provides strength around the basket, the area from which scoring opportunities are most efficient. It is the essence of simplicity.

This defense has great strategic value. It keeps the middle jammed to make it difficult for teams that have an exceptional pivot man. It is effective against screening plays and patterns. It keeps four men in the basket area at all times in order to have good position for rebounding.

All of the preceding attributes of this defense are also characteristic of the standard zone defenses. With these strong zone advantages, we still do not lose the advantage of pressing the man with the ball to force mechanical and judicative errors.

As in the preceding man-to-man defenses, each player is assigned to a player on the opponent team. His instructions remain the same—"Stop him." The primary difference is that only the man with the ball is pressed. The other four players loosen up on their men and drop toward the basket area.

For guarding the man with the ball we stress the following points:

1. Do not over-guard your man.
2. Never let him drive.
3. Let him take the long shot, when he is out of ordinary shooting range, unless he is having an exceptional night.
4. After the offensive man has used his dribble, press him tight and make him do something with the ball, if he is in shooting range.
5. Never allow him to get a rebound after his shot. Block him.

The assignment for the players, other than the one who is guarding the man with the ball, is to drop toward the foul lane and circle. We demand that each of the four men have at least one foot within this area and one foot outside of it. Figure 10 illustrates the position of the players using the drop back defense.

The players do not go to any set or predetermined posi-tion. This position is determined solely by the location of the man to whom they are assigned. When a man receives a pass, the player who is assigned to him, picks him up. The player who was guarding the man who passed the ball, drops back to the portion of the foul lane that is be-tween his man and the basket. It is obvious that the offen-sive players will be ever moving from one side of the foul lane and circle to the other side with their respective op-ponents. If all of the offensive players should move to the same side of the foul line, all four defensive men would move there also.

This defense may be used in conjunction with any of the other three man-to-man pressing defenses. However, the

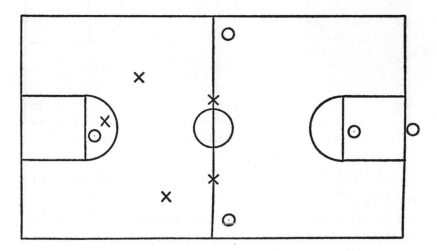

FIGURE 9. Basic Formation for the Half Court Press.

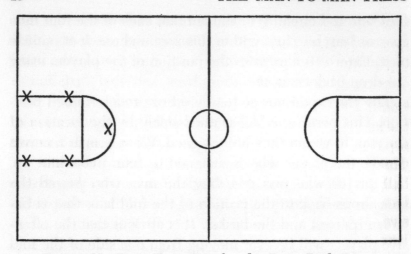

FIGURE 10. Basic Formation for the Drop Back Press.

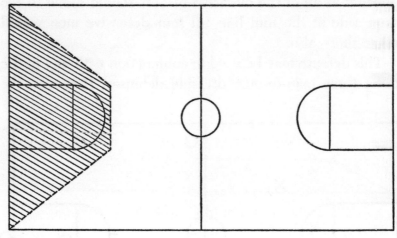

FIGURE 11. Defensive Area for Our Modified Drop Back.

drop back defense cannot be used until the ball moves into the forward court.

One other way of adjusting this defense is shown in Figure 11. This variation is for use, mainly, when the opposing team is shooting well outside and when they have been successfully screening in the corners and outside the foul lane and circle. This type of defense might well be called the quarter-court press. Notice in Figure 11 that the main difference between the drop back and this variation is merely the expansion of the defensive area.

The man with the ball is pressed rather tightly and the man that is nearest the ball on each side is guarded rather closely, unless they are outside of the defensive area.

If the ball is on one side, the defensive man (the off-side man) on the opposite side drops in toward the basket where he is expected to rebound any shot from the side.

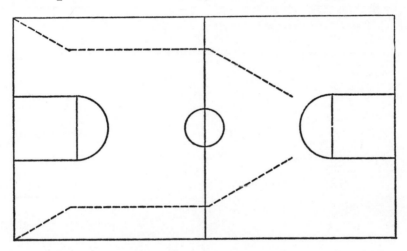

FIGURE 12. Where We Like to Keep the Dribbler.

We have one strict rule for all man-to-man defenses in the forward court. This rule is to keep the man with the ball out of the middle of the floor. Figure 12 illustrates the paths where the dribbler should be forced by the defense.

When an offensive guard is allowed to take the ball to the middle of the floor, he has options on each side and down the middle. If he is influenced down the side to the corner, he is limited to a small portion, where the only option should be to go back out the same way he came in. The defense, in order to keep the dribbler from passing inside, overplays all men inside of the dribbler.

After the man with the ball has been driven into the corner, he must be stopped completely or turned back up the side line. When you keep the man on the side, it gives us more defensive strength next to the ball, in that it allows our off-side man to drop into the basket area. If properly employed, this principle will always make your defense much tougher to crack.

5

THE DIAMOND ZONE
PRESS

The Diamond zone press defense has been one of our steadiest and most dependable. We spend more time in this defense than in any other back court or primary defense. It can be used for long periods of time where many of the primary defenses cannot. This defense does not have the color and appeal that some of our presses have but it is effective. The Diamond Zone Press is not designed to steal the ball every time, but to constantly harass a team and force it into mistakes. It is unique in that it allows our defense to overplay their men for the interception and still have them covered in case they break away.

There are several variations of this defense as there are of most of them. One is the 21A.

THE 21A PRESS

Each player must always be alert and on his toes in order to thwart an attempt to pass to their man. This is one of the things that can never be allowed. The pass in must be a long one, at least to the back of the foul circle.

This type of defensive alignment will tend to throw any opponent off stride. It tends to disorganize an organized team. It only takes several steals, interceptions, or turnovers of any type to hurt the "esprit de corps" of any team.

When our team shoots, we follow with a minimum of three men rebounding. If the opponent team uses the fast break, we use four men rebounding. As the ball goes through the basket, X^4, our slowest forward, immediately takes the man who will attempt to throw the ball in from out of bounds. In guarding this man, he should favor the man's throwing side. The hands should always be moving in the man's face in order to harass him. The important thing to remember is not to let him throw the straight baseball pass. This pass is too fast and accurate. It may beat our defensive man to its receiver. We want him to throw the high or lob pass or a bounce pass. These are the slowest passes and are the least efficient against our particular defenses. Naturally, X^4 should block the pass if he can.

Forward X^3 is our fastest forward and after the basket is scored, he covers the area to the left of the basket on defense. Figure 13 illustrates the zone that is the responsibility of X^3. In this zone he plays the closest man to the ball that is in this area. If, after the basket, there is no man to be seen in his area, he drops back until he finds a man. With a quick look, however, he can soon find what area is flooded. If the extra man is in someone else's area, he must move into this area and take him. X^3 overplays his man at all times. In this defense, we always play between the ball and our man or to the side and in front of our man. The main object is to make the offensive man cut away from the basket, thus demanding a longer pass. This gives the defensive man more time to get under the pass.

X^2, our slowest or largest guard, moves into the zone to the right of the basket after we score. His territory is shown by the shaded area in Figure 14. This is his zone and he plays the nearest man to the ball. His assignment is identical with that of X^3's, only on the opposite side.

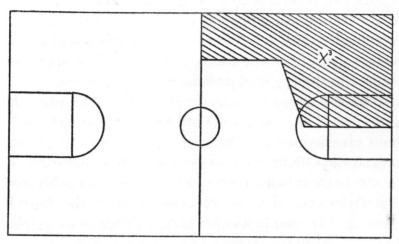

FIGURE 13. Responsibilities of X^3.

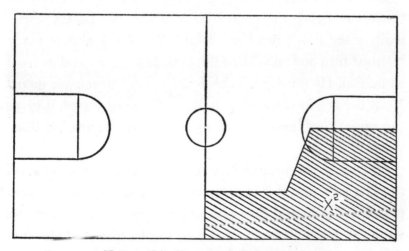

FIGURE 14. Responsibilities of X^2.

X^1 is our fastest guard and our defensive quarterback. He must be a quick, determined, and intelligent individual. His first job is to drop back and cover against the long pass. He covers until our center recovers to take over and release him. In watching back he should watch the man who is taking the ball out of bounds to see how far back he must play. If the man out of bounds is in a square stance, he may loosen up because it is difficult to throw a long pass from a square stance. However, if he is in a position (staggered stance) to throw a long pass, he must be cautious.

If for any reason X^1 is caught under the basket when the shot is made he must assume the duties of guard X^2 and X^2 must play his position. This saves confusion and maintains organization under all circumstances. After releasing, X^1 must take the man in his area. If there is no man in his area, it is obvious that there are two men in some other area. If there are two men in another area, X^1 must move quickly to pick up the second man.

X^5, the center, is usually the largest and slowest boy on the team. Being the center he is under the basket, especially after a shot has been taken. When the shot is made he must turn and run down the floor just as fast and as hard as he can. He must get back fast in order to release guard X^1. If the center is too slow in releasing your guard, it gives the opposition time to find an open man. Figure 16 illustrates X^5's zone.

Of course, the main objective of this defense is to pick off the first pass and if it is properly executed with the correct personnel, it should give you quite a few interceptions. Its strongest point, though, is if you fail to intercept the first pass, you still can maintain fair defensive balance. Recov-

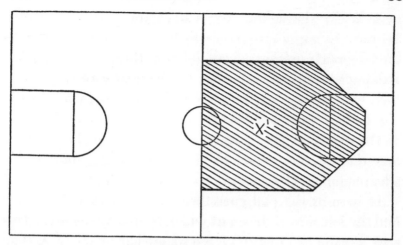

FIGURE 15. X¹.

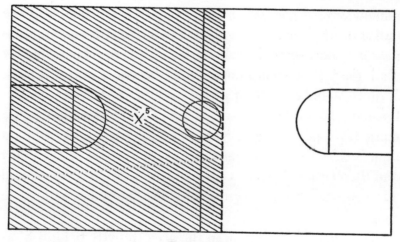

FIGURE 16.

ery time on this defense is not as great as it is on some of
the other presses.

THE 21B PRESS

The first variation of 21A press is 21B. Its basic formation is shown in Figures 17 and 18. This defense is used

periodically throughout our games for various strategic reasons. Its main purpose is to force the opponents into fundamental mistakes. These defenses thrive on bad passes, walking violations, and other mechanical errors.

As you can see, we have taken the man, X^4, who usually guards the man out of bounds, and placed him on the court on the left hand side. This gives us a numerical advantage over the opposing team. However, in order to obtain this advantage, we allow an uncontested pass-in.

As soon as the ball goes through the basket, X^3 moves into the left side of the court which is his starting area. This area, as shown in Figure 17, is a somewhat smaller area than in 21A press. The offensive man in X^3's area must be overplayed toward the ball. Staying between the man and the ball and being close enough to the man to still intercept the pass is a most difficult task. Again, this is to force a long or a lob pass. If X^3's man cuts across the court into X^2's area, X^3 must maintain a tight guard on him at all times. No defensive man switches any player who moves across the court from left to right. Switches take place only when a man breaks from a corner toward the middle of the court and then either X^4 or X^1 would pick him up. In short, X^3 and X^2 must not let their men receive the first pass, at least in their area.

X^1 takes up his position in the area directly behind X^2 as shown in Figure 18. After the basket is made, X^1's first responsibility is to protect against the long pass. He must stay back until center X^5 gets back to release him. This must be a swift exchange so that X^1 may assume his defensive assignment as quickly as possible. X^1 takes any man in his area and plays him tight, but does not overplay him. If there is no man in his area, he looks to X^2's area and if there is an extra man there, he takes him. If there is no man in the area, X^1 drops in behind the foul circle. From here he can move as quickly right as left. His assignment now is to observe where help might be needed. Also, the responsibility of picking up loose men rests with him.

X^4's assignment is identical with that of X^1.

If the offensive team brings up all four men, center X^5 follows to midcourt. If he goes beyond midcourt, he must have a very good chance for an interception to justify it. His duty is still to protect against the long pass.

The interceptions on this defense are usually made by X^1 and X^4. When X^3 and X^2 play between the ball and their man, the offensive man sometimes pivots and cuts down the floor for a lead pass. X^1 and X^4 are in perfect positions to anticipate this and to be there for the interception.

When the first pass is completed by the offensive team, we automatically drop into a predetermined defense. Usually, it is a man-to-man defense. When this occurs, the defensive man who is guarding the man with the ball must

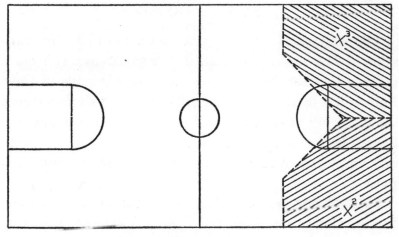

FIGURE 17.

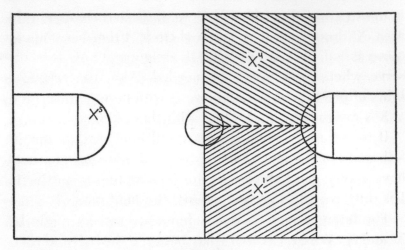

<figure>FIGURE 18.</figure>

try to contain him. Play him loose enough to encourage him to dribble instead of passing down the court. This will give you time to get set up defensively.

Figures 19 through 22 show some situational occurrences with this type of defense and how a team reacts to them.

21A TRAP DEFENSE

The most colorful and sometimes the most effective variation of 21A zone press is the 21A trap defense. It is not a defense that can be used over extended periods of time. Rather, it is used sparingly at different intervals throughout the game just as are most of the primary zone pressing defenses. It is a "surprise" type of defense and if it is properly employed, it may cause the opponents to lose their poise.

Most of our defenses that are variations of other defenses, closely resemble the "parent" defense. 21A trap defense has basically the same formation in its first stage.

Figure 23 illustrates the basic formation of the 21A trap. You can see that it is very similar to 21A defense. This increases the effect of the element of surprise.

First, you will notice that X^1 and X^3 have changed places. Our two fastest and best defensive men must be in the two corners. The bulk of the responsibility, however, rests upon the shoulders of X^4. His is the most difficult assignment. The first objective is to influence the man who is throwing the ball in, to pass it into one corner or the other. Usually it does not make too much difference which corner it is thrown to, but, sometimes we will want the ball thrown into a specific corner for some strategic reason.

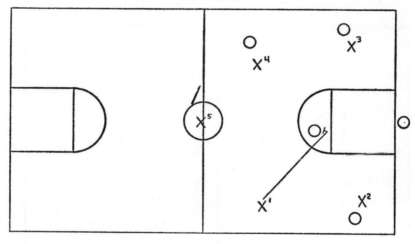

FIGURE 19.

On this particular defense, X^4 must get back quickly after the basket to defend against the long pass. Usually this is the job of X^1. X^4 has the same responsibility as any player who is assigned to protect against the long pass. Center X^5 must get back down the floor as quickly as he can.

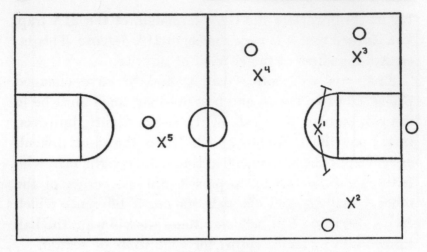

FIGURE 20.

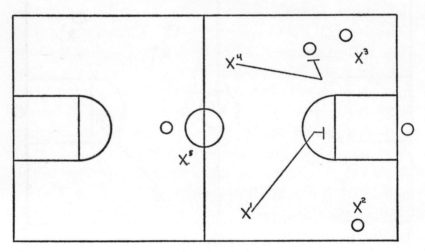

FIGURE 21.

X^3 has the key position in this defense. His assignment is to contest the pass in from out of bounds. This defense will function only if the ball is passed in to one corner or the other. When the man out of bounds appears to be concentrating on a target down the floor and not on one of

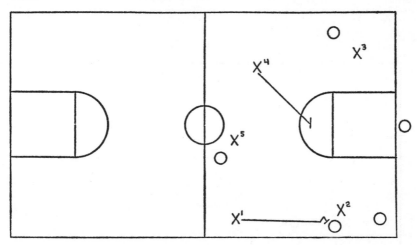

FIGURE 22.

the corners, X^3 has to force his attention to the corners by defensing him hard on his front side. X^3 does not play as close to the baseline as is usually done in guarding the man out of bounds. The distance that you keep between the man out of bounds and his guard depends upon the speed of X^3. On occasion, X^3 will overplay the man out of bounds to the left or right side in order to force the pass to a certain side. Many times one man on the opponent team will be weaker than another. We want the passing to go to this individual, if it is at all possible.

When the ball is passed to the corner, X^3 must advance toward the receiver as quickly as he possibly can. Figure 24 demonstrates a pass in to the right corner. Notice how X^3 moves to the man. X^3 and X^2 make up the "trap" in the corner. They must not allow their man to pass out of this double team. One major danger that must be guarded against is allowing the dribbler to split between X^3 and X^2. When this is allowed to happen, an easy basket usually results.

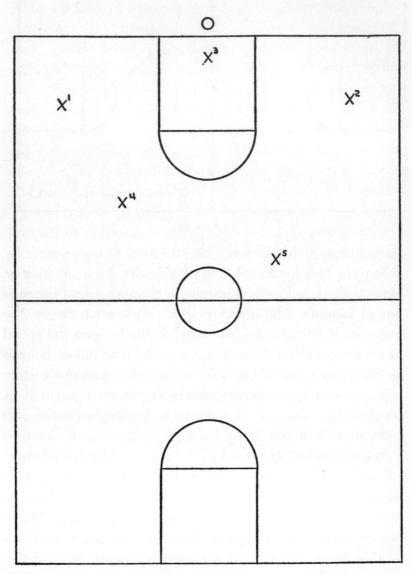

FIGURE 23. Basic Formation of 21A Trap.

X^2 and X^3 play loose on their men and allow them to go to the corner area unharassed. If they try to go some place other than this "free" area, they must meet fierce resistance by the defense. Usually after being pressed tightly, they will be more than glad to go to the area where they may receive a free pass. X^1 and X^2 will play behind and to the side of their respective men while they are in the corner areas. Each man is played on a man-to-man basis until the pass in. Figure 26 illustrates each man's position after the pass in. X^1 must move over and take up a position in the foul lane or circle after the pass in goes to the opposite corner. This is to prevent a return pass to O^1. O^3, in the trap, now has less than ten seconds in which to advance the ball across the mid-court line. The one man whom we leave open is O^2, who is in the opposite corner from O^3. It has been my experience that the man in the trap tries to throw the long down court pass to X^4 or X^5. This, naturally, is the easiest pass to intercept because of the time it takes in reaching its intended target. Also, many of these passes go astray and out of bounds. If O^3 should complete a pass to O^2 in the opposite corner, we still have enough time to recover and adjust. When any pass is thrown by O^3, we are automatically out of 21A trap defense. We usually switch to a straight 55A man-to-man or one of our defenses that fall back to mid-court. Regardless of which defense we switch to, the man nearest the receiver picks him up and slows him down. He should not press him so tightly that he throws a pass, but loose enough to encourage him to dribble. As long as he is dribbling, we are adjusting. If he passes quickly, he may find our momentary weakness.

If the pass from the man out of bounds goes to the left side, the assignments are just the opposite.

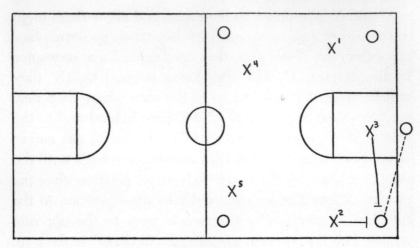

FIGURE 24.

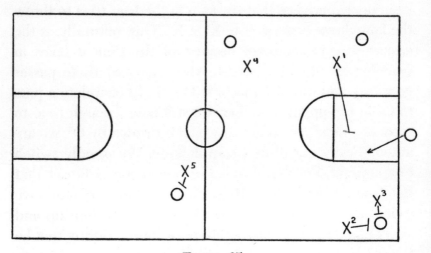

FIGURE 25.

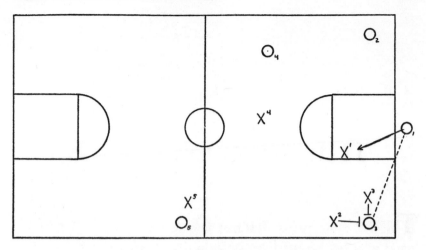

FIGURE 26. Right Side Pass In.

6

THE 3-2 ZONE PRESS

The 3-2 zone press defense is a versatile one. It can be used as a backcourt trap or as a dropback defense.

As a front court defense, it is very strong against outside shooting teams. Good rebounding position and ideal fast break position are several of its virtues. If it has a weakness, it is in the pivot area.

THE 3-2 ZONE TRAP

The backcourt 3-2 zone trap defense will be discussed first. Its basic formation is shown in Figure 27.

After we have scored, X^1, our fastest guard, drops back to midcourt to protect against the long pass. He must be certain before he releases and goes to his defensive assignment. Due to X^1's important role in the backcourt presses and traps, it can be readily seen why our center must be a real hustler in getting back after a score. X^1 is also responsible for closing the trap in this backcourt trap defense. When the man out of bounds is preparing to throw the ball in, the front line, X^1, X^2, and X^3 must influence his pass by their position as much as possible. The man who must be kept from receiving a pass is the opponent in the area of

X^4. If we can keep this one man from receiving the pass, we can be assured that the pass will be a short one. Our three front men line up with the foul line and the first pass

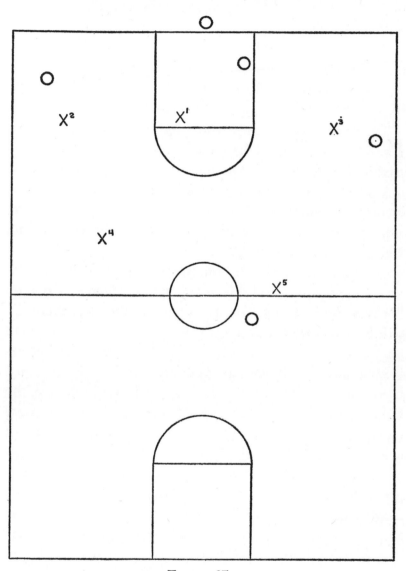

FIGURE 27.

should be inside of this position. If the first pass goes to either corner, X^1 goes to that corner to double team with X^2 (Figure 28). If the pass does not go to the corner, the three front men tighten up toward the middle to attempt to force the dribbler to go or pass to one corner or another (Figure 30). X^1 goes to the same corner as the pass. After the pass goes to the corner, X^2, will attempt to rush the receiver hard and fast to make him turn his back. By this time, X^1 has had ample time to arrive to close the trap.

The main concern after the trap has closed is the man who threw the ball in bounds. If he breaks fast after the pass in, it is possible that he may get a return pass from the man inside of the trap. This should never happen if X^1 and X^2 do a good defensive job, but if it does, the guard on the side opposite the side of the pass in (X^3) has to take him. This is shown in Figure 29. X^3 must play this man wherever he goes on the court. The toughest assignment in this defense belongs to X^4 who is more or less a floater. He is on his own. After the opponent player is in the trap, there are still two men unguarded with X^4 being the only free man on defense. He must use his own discretion as to his defensive position. If the two men are widely split, he must favor the one nearest the ball and if they are both near the ball, he should split between them. He should be near enough to reach either man in time to deflect or intercept a pass. This will demand a man who will hustle all the time.

The primary job of X^5 is to protect the front court and to guard the man to whom he is assigned. In this defense, he must remain very alert due to the fact that the man in the trap will, many times, lob a wild, long pass out of the double team. If he does, X^5 will be in a good position to get under many of them. X^5, however, should never leave his

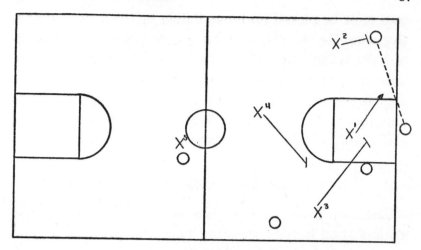

FIGURE 28.

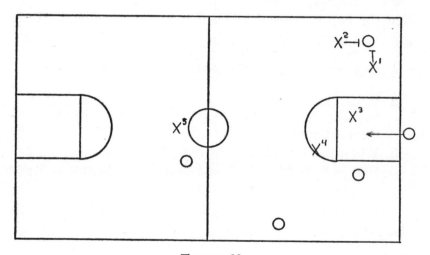

FIGURE 29.

man in an attempt for an interception unless he is 100 per cent sure that he has it.

If the offensive team does manage to complete the pass out of the double team, we try to drop back as quickly as possible. The opponent who receives the pass out of the trap must be picked up immediately by the nearest defensive man. He must be kept busy enough to alter his progress down the floor so that the rest of the team will have time to recover. Figure 31 illustrates the positions that our players drop to. They retreat to the same positions every time there is reason to drop back. This keeps us organized and instills a feeling of security among the players.

DROP BACK 3-2 PRESS

The drop back 3-2 press is a very good defense to use against good outside shooting teams. It provides a good position for rebounding and for the fast break. The main difference between the 3-2 zone press and the regular zone is that the ball is pressed when it is in any zone area. Here are some of the basic rules for playing the 3-2 zone press:

1. Press the man with the ball when he is in your area. Ignore any other offensive man in your area.
2. When there is no one in your area, find the area that has more than one man in it and move in to pick up the extra man.
3. When there is more than one man in your area and none of them have the ball, you will play the man nearest the ball.

Figure 32 illustrates the basic formation and Figure 33 shows each man's zone or territory for which he is responsible.

X^1, our fastest guard, plays the middle position on the front line. This outer half of the foul circle represents an area that must be protected at all cost. Once the opponents have broken past this defensive position, the whole defense is shattered. Of course, this is true to a certain extent of each of the five positions in this defensive alignment.

PLATE 3. *Typical Rebounding Drill.*

PLATE 4. *A Fine Example of Rebounding Position.* (Notice every man has blocked.)

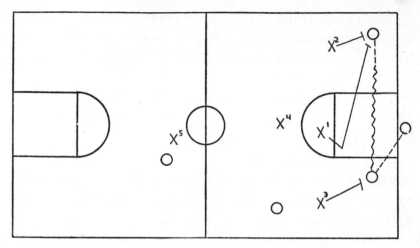

FIGURE 30.

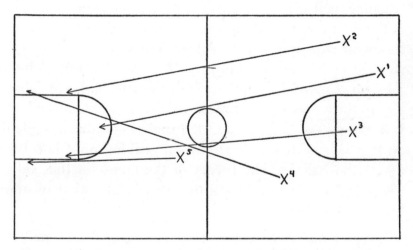

FIGURE 31. Dropping Back After Completed Pass Out of Trap.

Guard X^1 must never advance further than the back of the circle or retreat behind the foul line. Essentially, this semi-circle is his area. Naturally, we allow a certain amount of decision to rest with the individual player. Under rare circumstances, X^1 will be forced to leave this area, but this is a last resort. If the offensive team employs a pattern that uses a pivot man on the foul line, X^1 must prevent the pass from being thrown in to him, even if it means dropping a step from the foul circle.

X^2 and X^3 are the wingmen on the front line and it is their responsibility to prevent shooting from the sides of the court. Figures 34 and 35 graphically describe X^3's movements when the man with the ball moves down the sideline toward the corner. As the dribbler reaches the corner area, X^5 must pick him up and relieve X^3, who must then move back to his own area.

Many teams collapse these two wingmen when the ball is thrown into the pivot area, but we feel that when these wingmen collapse, they are leaving the men on their side of the floor unguarded for a return pass and an unopposed shot. Our wingmen never collapse. We let one of the back men, X^4 or X^5, take care of the pivot area. This gives him (the pivot man) less options with the ball and will cause him to throw poor passes occasionally. Also, when the ball is in the outside area around the foul circle, the wingman on that side of the floor assumes a position on a line between the ball and the corner of the court on that side. The wingmen are cautioned to be especially alert on the following points:

1. *Never* under any circumstances allow a man to drive around you.
2. Always keep your hands at least shoulder high.
3. Do not try to steal the ball or the dribble, but concentrate on good sound defensive maneuvers.
4. After a shot, always block out the man in your area and then go for the ball.
5. Talk on defense. Let your teammates know what is happening in your area.

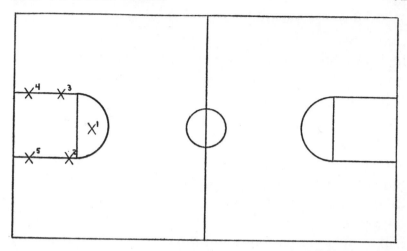

FIGURE 32. The Basic Formation of the "3-2" Zone.

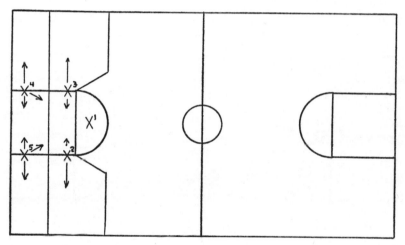

FIGURE 33. The Five Areas of the "3-2" Zone.

The two back men, X^4 and X^5, have the largest zone of any of the other three defensive players. They must cover both of the corners, the baseline and the foul lane area. We like to think of these two men's movements as though they were both tied to opposite ends of a ten foot piece of rope.

If X^5 advances toward his corner three steps, X^4 also takes
three steps in the same direction. These two must be a
highly mobile and adaptable unit. They work as one man.
Against a high pivot man one of the back men moves up
behind him and the opposite man moves to a position ap-
proximately under the basket so that he may move to either
side quickly. Figure 36 shows a high pivot, but with a
strong right side for the offense. X^5, then, does not drop
under the basket, but plays toward this strong side. Figure
37 shows the simple moves of X^4 and X^5 when the ball is
located in the corner. Figures 38 and 39 demonstrate the
ball in different positions and the corresponding defensive
adjustment.

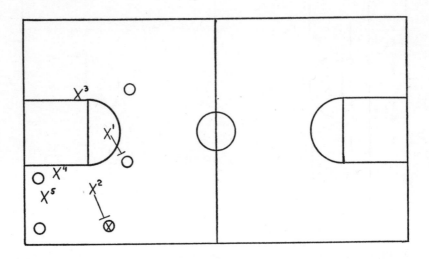

FIGURE 34. The Movements of the Wingmen.

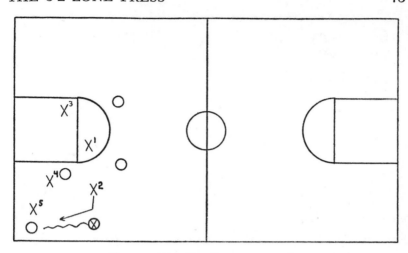

FIGURE 35. The Corner Switch.

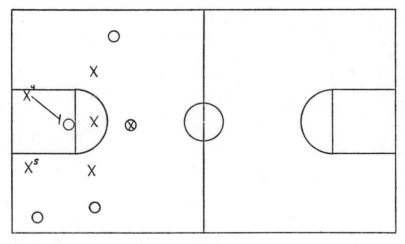

FIGURE 36. The Movements of the Backmen Against a High Pivot.

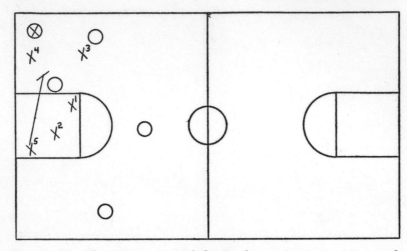

FIGURE 37. The Movements of the Backmen Against a Man in the
Corner.

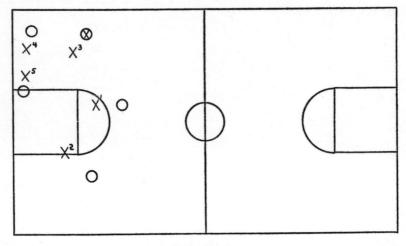

FIGURE 38.

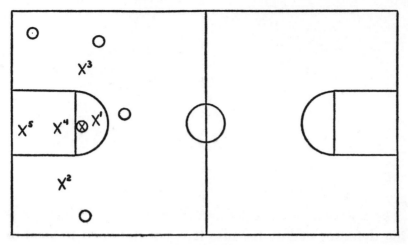

FIGURE 39.

7

THE 2-3 ZONE PRESS

The 2-3 zone press is different from the rest of our pressing defenses mainly because it is not designed to steal or intercept the ball. We use it primarily to force the opposing team to slow down their offensive attack. There are times when, being several points ahead, we would like to slow down the tempo of the game in order to apply pressure to the opponents. We want them to move the ball outside and shoot outside, also.

In this defense, we never contest those passes that are going outside or those that do not represent a scoring threat. But when a pass is thrown inside or to the corner area, we put up fierce resistance. This same principle also applies to the dribble. As long as the opponent player is dribbling the ball outside or is in a non-critical area, he can go in peace. The instant that he tries to get into an area where a high percentage shot may be taken, we pressure him and allow him to go anywhere but toward the inside. It is a curious thing, but when a team realizes that we are attempting to make them slow down their offense, they seem to be twice as eager to speed it up, the result being forced shots and forced passes. It is a well disciplined and organized team that can successfully combat this urge. The principal difference between this defense and a standard 2-3 zone defense is in the way it functions as a unit. We play this defense out a little higher and, generally, in a more open fashion. This type of play results when attempted in the pivot area, and consequently gives us more opportunity for interceptions.

After scoring, our team gets down the floor quickly and sets up the defense. Figure 40 illustrates the basic defensive positions of the 2-3 zone press. X^3, X^4, and X^5 are responsible for any rebound that comes off of the board except for those that bounce long and these are the responsibility of our guards.

Guards X^1 and X^2 never move out of the circle when the ball is directly beyond the foul circle unless the man with the ball is a very high percentage shooter. They do move out when the ball is at medium distance to either side of the foul circle. Figure 41 shows the ball in this position and also illustrates the area in which we will allow the dribbler to go unchecked. He must be driven to the sideline or forced to go back outside. Notice, too, that X^2 moves over into X^1's area when X^1 is forced to move out.

X^4 and X^5 are the two side rebounders and their areas extend from the corners to the foul line. They must position themselves in front of any opponent who is in the foul lane or near the foul lane in their zone. On this defense, we will generally let the opponents take the very deep corner shot unless he starts hitting too well. We especially like to get one of their big men in the corner for he is easier to block out there. The man in the corner must not drive around the baseline. This is the responsibility of X^4 and X^5. If the ball moves into the area of X^4 or X^5, they must play the man rather tightly until they have forced him out to

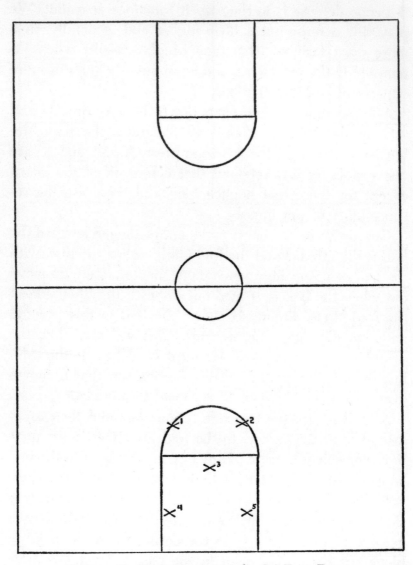

FIGURE 40. Basic Formation for 2-3 Zone Press.

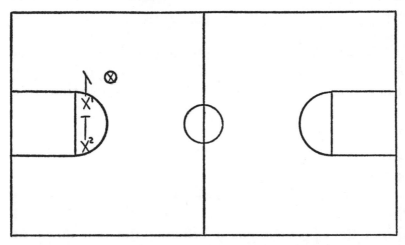

FIGURE 41. Movements of the Guards in the "2-3" Press.

where his shot will be of some length. At this point, using their own discretion as to the location of this spot, they should loosen up enough to allow the man to look for someone to receive his pass. Figure 43 shows X^4 defensing the ball in the corner. Note how X^5 has sagged into the position vacated by X^4. When X^5 and X^4 are shifted over one position in this manner, X^2 drops back from the foul circle and will rebound from this side in the event of a shot from the corner.

X^3, our fastest forward, plays the center position. It is his job to stay in front of the man (or men) cutting in and out of the foul lane. X^3 should not go out of the foul lane more than a step or two. He must also play any opponent who moves into the high pivot. Figure 42 shows two basic defensive positions that X^3 is called upon to assume under certain circumstances. X^3 does not have to worry when the ball is on the side because he has plenty of help sagging in from other positions. Figure 43 shows how each man moves against an actual offensive situation.

THE "2-3" CORNER TRAP

This 2-3 corner trap uses the same defensive lineup as the 2-3 zone defense. The main difference is that we play it in a more spirited manner. It is like all of our traps from the standpoint that we do not want to give the opponents too much opposition until we get them where we want them. As the topical heading might suggest, we want them in the corners.

Our guards, X^1 and X^2, must force the ball to go toward the corner by pure influence by their position. Figure 44 shows the opponent guard bringing the ball down the strong side. Notice how X^2 posts out to influence the guard on down that side and to discourage him from moving toward the middle of the court. X^1, at the same time, is still laying back to keep from alarming the guard with the ball. Figure 45 finds the guard passing to O^1 on the side. X^1 slides over to take O^1 and at the same time, X^4 is moving down the baseline in anticipation of the pass from O^1 to

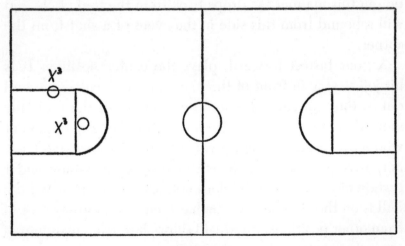

FIGURE 42.

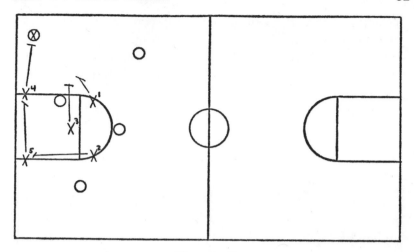

FIGURE 43.

the man in the corner. X^4 must not be close enough to the corner man to prevent O^1 from passing it. X^3 has moved in front of the only other logical receiver and X^2 has moved over to the area vacated by X^1. X^5 remains back in the foul lane to cover any lob pass.

When O^1 passes to the man in the corner (Figure 46), X^1 slides quickly from O^1 to form half of the double team. X^4 represents the other half as he comes down the baseline. The moves of X^1 and X^4 must be simultaneous. X^2 moves in to intercept any quick return pass to O^1 and X^5 plays for any wild or lob pass.

After the trap is sprung in the corner, it is strictly up to X^1 and X^4. It is our contention if two men on one cannot prevent a good pass out then these two men are defensive players of the poorest type. Some of the basic rules for the double team are as follows:

1. Swarm the man with the ball.
2. Use your arms and hands. Keep them in his face and after the ball.

3. *Never* allow the man to split between you.

4. Do not get over enthusiastic and foul.

5. If the man throws a pass, make it a lob or a bounce
   pass. These are the slowest and the easiest passes to
   intercept.

6. After the pass, be prepared to recover on defense if it
   is completed. If it is not, move into the fast break pattern.

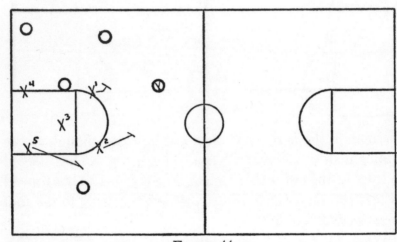

FIGURE 44.

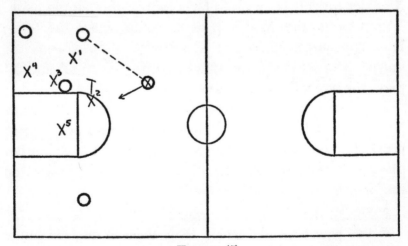

FIGURE 45.

We never tell our team what to do when a man escapes a trap. It is a sin for a man to escape. All good trapping defenses are controlled so that they operate at maximum efficiency. Disorganized traps usually lead to easy baskets.

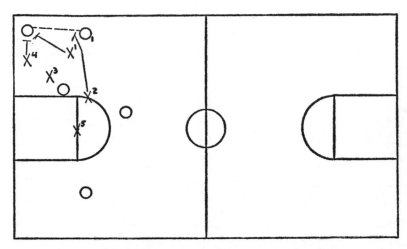

FIGURE 46. Corner Trap from the Left Side.

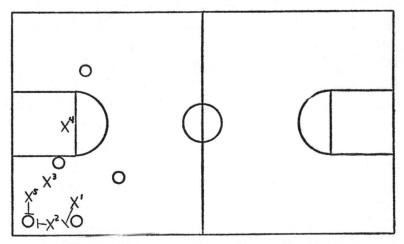

FIGURE 47. Corner Trap from the Right Side.

8

THE 2-1-2 ZONE PRESS

The 2-1-2 pressing defense is used almost exclusively as a half court defense. This is a variation of the many half court defenses that we fall back into after a team has cracked through our primary defense in the backcourt.

This particular type of press discourages the offensive team from attempting to slow down the game. Like all of the zone presses it tends to disorganize the team that is accustomed to using a pattern and play offense. This defense is not quite as risky as a full court press so it can be used when you feel that you need to press but do not want to chance a full court press. This type of defense will often cause a young or inexperienced player to crack under the pressure.

Figure 48 illustrates the basic formation of the 2-1-2 press. The three front men will act as a single unit. They must be perfectly coordinated in their actions. In order to coordinate these movements one of them must be designated as a captain. His responsibility will be that of calling the different attacks that this three-man unit will employ. The two back men also work as a unit. As you can see by Figure 48, the two front men must be your fastest men. Defensive prowess and good recovery ability are

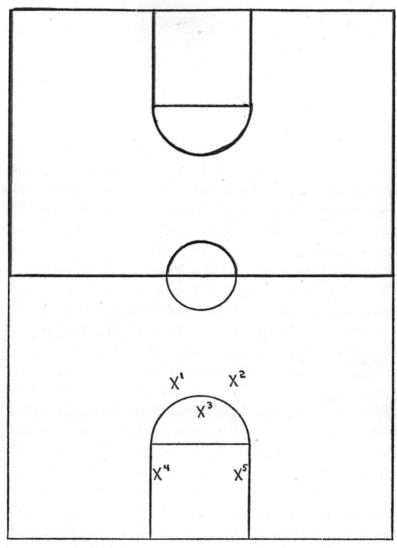

FIGURE 48. The Basic Formation of the 2-1-2 Pressing Defense.

prime requisites for this position. The middle man is actually the key man in this defense. It is he who must have
that extra sense that allows him to quickly diagnose play
situations and to anticipate passes. It is also important for
him to have good recovery ability. The back men should
be your two largest men. Usually the pivot man and the
largest forward make up this two man unit.

THE DROP BACK

After we have scored or the opponents have possession
of the ball, we drop back fast. After we get set up in the
positions shown in Figure 48, we wait until the opposing
guard brings the ball down the floor. When the guard
crosses mid-court, our two front men, X^1 and X^2, spread
out toward the men near the baselines. They do not go
all the way to the men on the side, but just close enough
to discourage the guard from passing to the side and also
to encourage him to advance down the middle. Once he
begins coming down the middle, X^1 and X^2 start moving
toward each other and should plan to meet this guard
just a step or two behind the foul circle. As the guard
reaches this position behind the foul circle, X^1 and X^2
rush him and put on the pressure. Figure 49 demonstrates
how X^1 and X^2 rush the guard. X^3, the middle man, now
must be very alert. Realizing the guard that is rushed
must pass the ball, he must try to anticipate the pass and
where it is being thrown. X^3, if it is possible, can shoot
the gap and intercept the pass. If he cannot do this, he
immediately rushes to the man who received the pass
(Figure 50). X^1, the man on the same side as the pass,
rushes to the pass receiver and doubleteams him. All of
this maneuver must be executed in a very swift and precise

manner. A pass to the side also influences the movements
of the back man on the opposite side which in this situation is X^5. He moves into the pivot area to protect and also

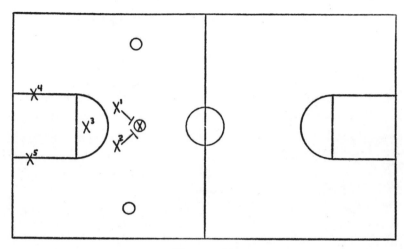

FIGURE 49.

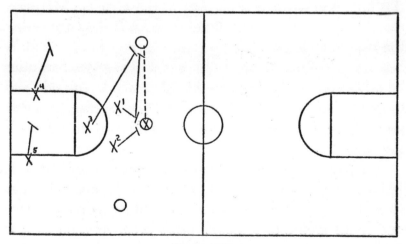

FIGURE 50.

to be alert for the lob pass. The doubleteam by X^3 and X^1 must follow these basic points:

1. Do not allow the man to go around your outside. Box him.
2. Harass him so tightly that you either steal the ball, tie him up, or force him to throw a bad pass.
3. Do not reach in, slap or in any way draw an uncalled for foul.
4. Keep your arms and hands high and keep them moving. This forces either a lob pass or a bounce pass.
5. Block his vision. Do not allow him to get a good look for a receiver.
6. Never allow the man to split between you. Keep yourself and your teammate's inside knees almost together.
7. After the pass, drop back as quickly as you can to the foul circle area.

When the first pass is made by the guard behind the foul circle, X^2 drops back to the foul circle on the side where the ball was passed. He overplays the first man in this area and if there is no man in the area, he overplays the closest man to the ball. This man, X^2, is shown covering the passer as he cuts for the basket in Figure 52. X^2 picks him up man for man after the pass and releases him after he advances into the area of X^4. X^4 moves to the side and overplays the first man in that area or cutting into that area. If there is no one in the area, he drops back toward the basket.

If a pass is completed, every man tries to get back to his area as quickly as possible. Occasionally, men will have to be switched or a defensive man will be forced to move out of his area into someone else's area. As soon as it is feasible, he should attempt to move back into position.

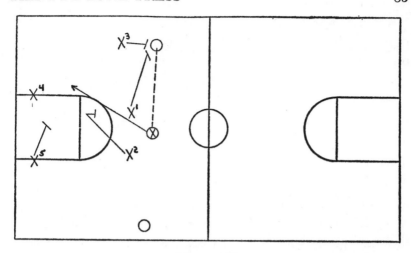

FIGURE 51.

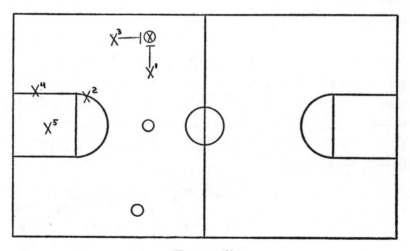

FIGURE 52.

VARIATION AIMED AT OPPOSING GUARD

Another variation of this defense will now be discussed. The advantage of it is that it looks to the approaching guard just like the defense discussed above. We usually have our defensive captain switch into this defense periodically to keep our play from becoming compulsive and obvious.

The basic formation of this variation (Figure 53) is identical to the defense previously discussed. Rushing the opposing guard several times makes him begin to get cautious. When he gets cautious, he passes as soon as he detects X^1 and X^2 starting toward him. As Figure 54 shows, X^1 and X^2 start their rush, but veer off at right angles before they close on him. If he has been passing early, either X^1 or X^2 should pick off a pass because the guard believes they are going for him and passes without too much caution. In case he does not pass, X^3 holds his position and takes him if he decides to advance. If he does not have a dribble left, X^3 will press him tightly and then go to the pass. Figure 55 shows this maneuver. When X^1 and X^2 flare toward the men on the sides, they go only until the pass is made. If the pass is completed to one side or another, X^3 follows the pass for the double team and the opposite guard drops to the foul circle. Then when the pass is thrown, the doubleteam can now once again be employed (Figure 56).

Corner Trap from 2-1-2 Zone Press

The corner trap from the 2-1-2 zone is one of the strongest types of traps. We like to force the ball into the corner and then doubleteam that man. We use exactly the same formation as in the last two defenses. The main difference is that in this defense we do not press too tightly outside. This is to discourage the dribble and to keep the ball moving toward the corner.

As the opponent guard approaches the back of the foul

circle, X^1 and X^2 rush him as in the other defenses of this type. This maneuver will force him to pass to one side or another. In Figure 57 the pass is thrown to the left side of the court. The guard on the same side as the pass, which in this case is X^2, goes to the man who received the pass. X^3, the middle man, goes to that side also, but he does not press the man; rather, he assumes a position inside of the man to discourage him from driving. X^3 should apply just enough pressure to force the man to pass into the corner. When the pass goes to the corner man, X^5 moves quickly and arrives at the same time as the ball. His primary job is to stop the man and above all, prevent him from getting around the outside and driving the baseline. If he drives at all, it should be to the inside where there is help to be had. X^3 moves to the corner to doubleteam the man with the ball as soon as the pass is thrown. X^1 moves in to the foul circle on the side of the ball and protects this area. X^4, the back man on the right side, moves over to the foul lane to defend. The one open man is on the far side of the court. If a long pass should get to him, the defense should have ample time to adjust sufficiently to prevent any good scoring opportunity. Figure 58 shows each defensive man's position after the ball is trapped in the corner.

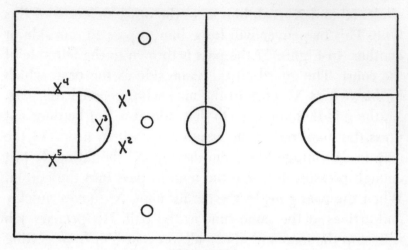

FIGURE 53.

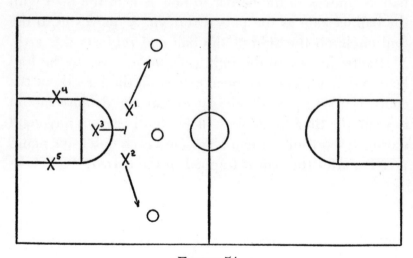

FIGURE 54.

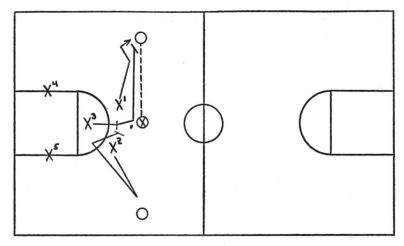

FIGURE 55.

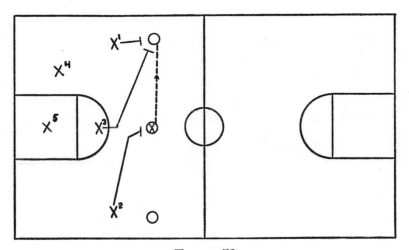

FIGURE 56.

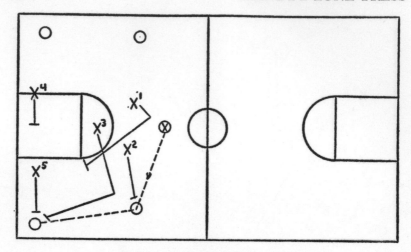

FIGURE 57. The Corner Trap.

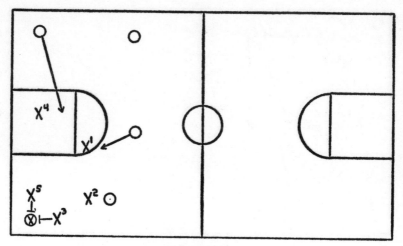

FIGURE 58. The Corner Trap Completed.

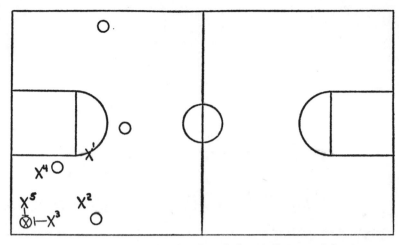

FIGURE 59. Offensive Overload and the Defensive Adjustment.

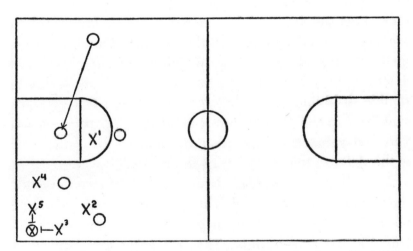

FIGURE 60. Notice How X^1 Splits Between the Last Two Men When They Are Close Together.

9

THE ZONE PRESS
TRAP DEFENSE

The zone trap when applied to a team that has not thoroughly scouted it, can be devastating. It is not a defense that can be used for an entire game. It is used in spots throughout a game. Usually, we have found it always good for several quick steals or jump balls. It also forces a team into many fundamental errors such as walking, double dribbling, or throwing away a pass. It represents that "ace up the sleeve" that is needed on occasion. When you find yourself behind near the end of the game, this is the defense that might turn the tables.

As in all of the pressing defenses, this defense demands the right type of personnel. The greatest need and absolute necessity in personnel are the guards. They must be of the true 100 per cent variety. The remaining members must also be very determined, hard working individuals and the center must be of the agile variety. It is only fair to point out that a single missed assignment will result in an easy basket for the opponents. The team must be well drilled in this defense to avoid any such happenings.

Figure 61 illustrates the starting formation of the zone trap defense. Since there are variations of this defense, we will call this one 32A.

32A TRAP

The first objective of the defense is to control the first pass from out of bounds. Notice that guards X^1 and X^2 are at three quarter court position and forwards X^3 and X^4 are at mid-court. This is to prevent the opposition from throwing the long pass. The pass in must be in close. If you begin a game in a tight full court press and harass the opposing guards, they will usually be more than happy to take the uncontested pass in.

After the pass in, allow the opponent guards to take as much time as they want. The amount of time that they use will loom as a factor in the success of his trap defense. Figure 62 illustrates, by the shaded area, where we want the guard to bring the ball. The half court is split in half and X^1 plays one half and X^2 the other. If the dribbler moves from one area to the other, the guards follow him only as far as the imaginary boundary that bisects the back court and then switch him to the other guard.

The role of the defensive guards is very important for the proper execution of this defense. The idea is to allow the opposing guards as much freedom as they want as long as they go to the shaded area. They cannot be allowed to bring the ball up the middle. They must be kept to the side line. The guards must not attempt to intercept pass or try to steal the ball. They tighten up on the dribbler only when he threatens to break out of the shaded area. The opposing guards must be made to feel secure and comfortable. Both defensive guards may even play close

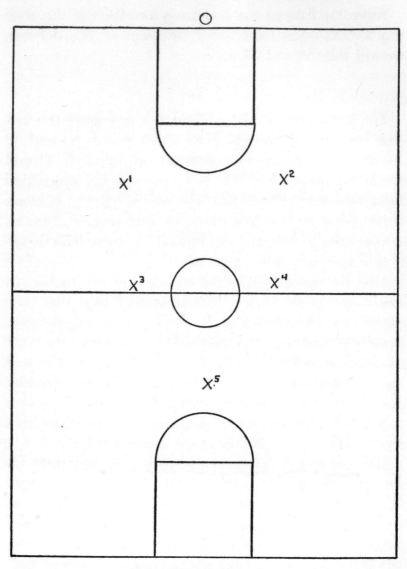

FIGURE 61.

together to prevent the ball from being brought up the middle. The dribbler has to be, literally, herded to the sideline.

After the dribbler has been forced to the sideline (Figure 63), X^2 drops back slightly to keep him from coming toward the middle. X^1 moves on him tightly enough to prevent him from leaving the sideline and breaking through to the middle.

The assignment of the forward is one of precise timing that is coordinated with the movements of the guard on his side. As the guard approaches the midcourt line, he must also approach at the same time. The movements of the guard and forward must be synchronized. Figure 64 shows the movements of the guard and forward for trapping on the left side of the floor. The forward's job is to stop the dribbler just as he takes *one step* across the ten second line. He must stop the dribbler in his tracks. The guard must arrive at exactly the same time to contain him on the side (Figure 65).

Now you must guard against the biggest single hazard of this trap defense. You must not allow the dribbler to split between X^3 and X^1. This will cause more damage than you can imagine if it should occur.

Once the man is in this trap, he is at the greatest possible disadvantage. His front and inside are blocked by the two defensive men, the back side is blocked by the ten second line, and his outside barrier is the baseline. The two defensive men must wave their hands in his face, attempt to get to the ball, and be so determined in their attack that he must throw a bad pass. Many times he will walk, step out of bounds, or step back over the ten second line before he has a chance to throw a pass. If a pass is completed, the responsibility rests solely with the two defensive men in the trap, X^1 and X^2. It is their job to see that the dribbler does not throw a good pass. Forward X^3

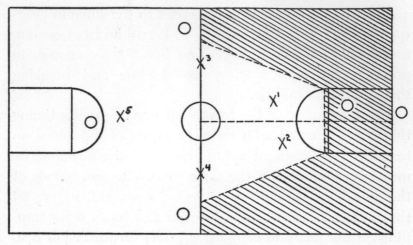

FIGURE 62.

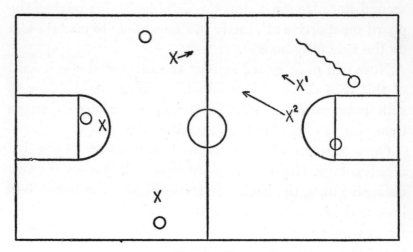

FIGURE 63.

should stop the dribbler with his hands high. This is to discourage the long pass and to encourage the bounce pass down the sideline. The bounce pass is a very slow pass and therefore allows our defensive man more time to move in and intercept. The most logical man for him to

PLATE 5. *A Good Example of 32A Trap.* (Notice the trap about to close in the background.)

PLATE 6. *The Guard Loosens up While the Other Slides Through.*

pass to is the man that forward X^3 has left open when he advances to mid-court to start the trap. We do everything possible to encourage the pass to this particular man. This is where the interceptions usually take place on this defense. The man who usually intercepts the pass is center X^5. He must time his move so that he gets to the spot in time to meet the dribbler's pass. The passer, guarded closely by two men, cannot see him coming from the side. Therefore, he usually thinks that he is passing to a man who is completely open. To him, it certainly appears that way.

In a movement that is synchronized with X^5's, X^4 moves quickly over to take the center that X^5 has left (Figure 66). The one man who is open is the man farthest from the ball. The dribbler should never be able to throw this kind of a pass with two men on him.

While this is occurring, guard X^2 has taken the remaining offensive guard and is playing him man-to-man to prevent him from receiving a pass. As soon as the trap is sprung, every man moves in front of the man they are guarding in order to intercept the pass, if it is thrown.

32B TRAP

A second variation of 32A trap is 32B. We were forced to develop this defense because of the offense developing effective techniques to use against 32A. After using 32A for some time, teams started finding weaknesses. One of these was to rush their center toward the trap (Figure 67) just as X^5 has left him to go to the sideline. This quick movement on his part did not allow X^4 enough time to reach him for the interception. Consequently, many of the passes to him were completed. The big hazard, however,

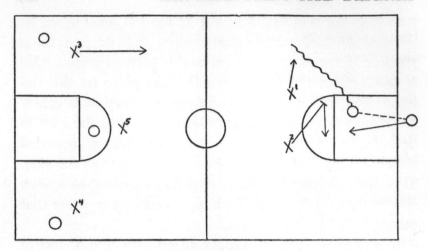

FIGURE 64.

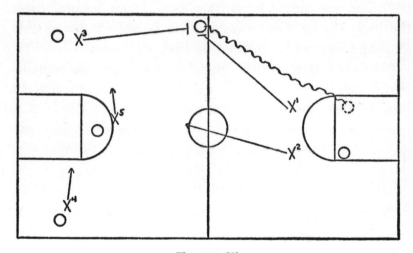

FIGURE 65.

was that when X^4 went out with the center, it left the whole foul lane open and the unguarded man would move into it. From this position, he could be seen much more easily by the man in the trap. He is also unguarded and alone in the whole basket area.

32B corrected this hazardous situation and saved our trap defenses. We switch in and out of 32A and 32B to keep the other team off guard. 32B defense operates exactly as 32A until the trap is sprung. Figure 68 illustrates the exact position of every man just before the change in to 32B. Notice that X^5 and X^4 are half way to their respective assignments. Just as the trap has closed and the dribbler has been checked, we execute a quick shift as shown in Figure 69. When the dribbler is just crossing the ten second line, X^2, who is the key man in this shift, loosens up on his guard and when the trap closes, he quickly drops back and takes the center that X^5 has just left. His job is to play for the pass. At exactly the same instant, guard X^1 drops back and takes the man that X^2 has just left. The importance of X^2's defensive shift can be readily seen. After X^1 drops out of the trap and back on the guard, X^3 plays the man in the trap in the most advantageous position. He should guard the man in a position that is on a diagonal line from the opposite corner.

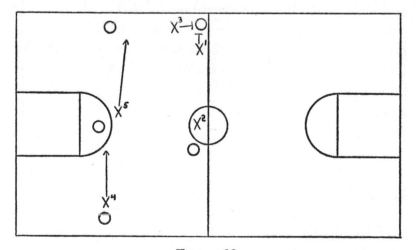

FIGURE 66.

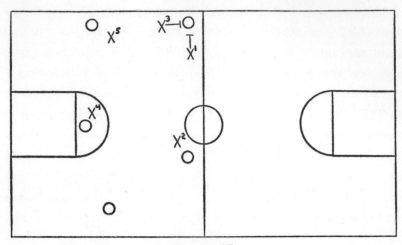

FIGURE 67.

One of the important factors in the success of this press is the work of X^4. In 32B after the shift, X^4 must immediately survey the situation. He must loosen toward the middle and find the extra man if he is not in his area.

The center, X^5, does not necessarily take the man in the corner, O^2. Center, X^5, must play a particular area or zone and must guard the man closest to the ball in his area. The center's area is shown by the dotted area in Figure 70. Figure 71 illustrates how a switch is made when a man breaks into an area where he is not usually found. There is one basic rule to follow when there are two men in the same zone. You must play the man who is nearest the ball. The last man to adjust must split the difference between the two remaining offensive men. However, he must never play so far out of the basket area that he cannot get back in time to check a man who receives a pass in this area.

In Figure 71 we have set up a hypothetical situation that very frequently occurs. Guard O^2 breaks around X^2 and cuts into the area where the interception is to be made. As he cuts around and away from his guard, X^5 must react instantly and move on him instead of O^3. This is his man now and he is responsible for not letting him receive a pass. X^4, who has left O^4, moves over to X^5. Under normal circumstances, X^4 must take O^5 but now he must split between O^3 and O^5 and cover both. He should be in such a position

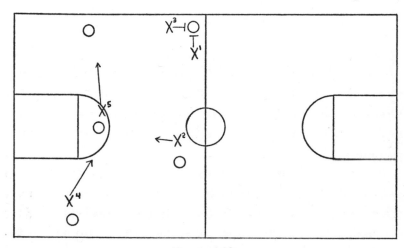

FIGURE 68.

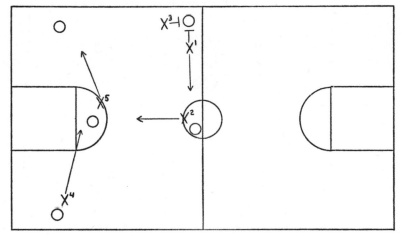

FIGURE 69.

that he can move quickly one way or the other. Sometimes O^3 will break to the basket or to the other side of the floor. In this situation, X^4 must use his own discretion as to whether or not O^3 is in position to receive a pass in scoring territory. However, if O^3 moves in behind O^5 or to the far side, we have X^4 play up on O^5 and depend on our forward and guard in the trap to prevent an accurate long pass.

So far everything has been viewed from the standpoint of the offensive team making a mistake. It is only fair to discuss those times when they do not. In football, if every man carried out his assignment successfully, every play would result in a touchdown. We know this does not happen too frequently due to the fact that human error is ever present.

If the man escapes the trap or in some way manages to get out of it, we have some secondary defense to which we resort. We never play to intercept the second pass. After the first pass from the trap, we usually drop into a man-to-man, drop back, or zone defense.

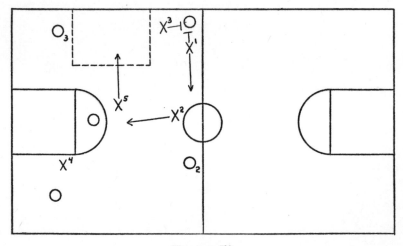

FIGURE 70.

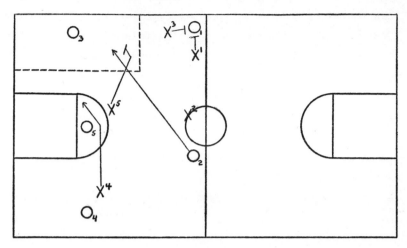

FIGURE 71.

10

THE PRESSING
ZONE DEFENSES

The pressing zone is quite often confused with the zone
press. The two types of defense operate on different the-
ories. The zone presses may be employed in any area of
the basketball court. There are no geographic restrictions
attached to a zone press whereas the pressing zones are
strictly reserved to the area of standard zone defenses.
Even at the extreme a pressing zone seldom covers more
than a half court area. The zone presses are much more
intrepid in nature than are the pressing zone defenses. For
instance, a pressing zone defense will not have a deliberate
trap play in its organization. Although in some variations
of a pressing zone we use a doubleteam occasionally, it is
not a calculated "trap" play. As opposed to the zone presses,
the pressing zones assignments for each man are more
clearly defined and do not leave as much decision upon the
individual player.

The difference between the pressing zone and a regular
zone is that you press the man with the ball tightly when
he is in your area. If he drives around you, he is bound to

move into another area and the man in that area will meet him and press him tightly again. This demands quick reaction and adjustment on the part of each player.

Four different types of pressing zones will now be discussed. Basically, the same principles are used for any pressing zone and only the individual areas and assignments are different.

THE 2-3 PRESSING ZONE

The basic formation of the 2-3 pressing zone is shown in Figure 72. The two guards are positioned in the front line usually no further advanced than the back of the foul circle. Undoubtedly, these two guards, X^1 and X^2, represent success or failure depending upon how well they hustle, move, and work together as a team. Unity and coordination between these two players is essential and vital. The 2-3 pressing zone is only as good as its guards. The ability to recover quickly is a valuable asset to all players that participate in this type of defense.

The three men who make up the back row of the 2-3 zone must also be well coordinated as an effective mobile unit. X^3, who plays the middle position in the back row should be the quickest and fundamentally the best player in the back row. This is only logical due to the fact that he is the one that has to adjust more often and has the least stable area of defense. This man will usually be your fastest forward. These qualities are essential for the purpose of defending a crucial area (pivot area) on the court and also for rebounding from the middle position on defense.

The two men on the wings of the back line should be the two largest men on the team. X^5, the center and probably the best rebounder, is positioned on the left side of the basket because more shots are taken from the right hand side of the court and therefore, we feel that the largest number of rebounds go to the left side of the basket. X^4 automatically is placed on the right side of the basket.

Each of these five men begins any defensive series with an assigned area. Figure 73 shows the individual area as-

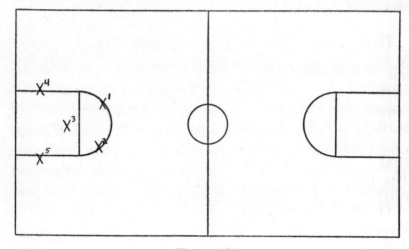

FIGURE 72.

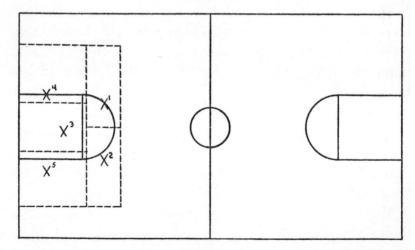

FIGURE 73.

signments for the 2-3 pressing zone. It must be kept in mind
that there are the individual areas, but that any player
may have to move into any other area if the offensive position of the opponent team demands it. It is obvious that if
two offensive men are in one defensive area another defensive man will have to leave his area to help out in this
area. The rest of the defense moves into the open areas in
the basket region and leaves open the area that is farthest
away from the man with the ball. Figure 74 illustrates this
by showing the adjustment for two offensive men in X^5's
area.

Now that the areas and adjustments have been worked
out, it is logical to discuss the principles used in the pressing
zone defenses.

1. Play the man in your area as tightly as you possibly
can. Forget about anyone else being in your area.
Your responsibility is the man with the ball.
2. Play him as long as he is in your zone, but switch
him when he moves into another zone.
3. After the man has been switched, drop back quickly
to your original starting position in your area.
4. Always be looking for an area next to your own that
has two offensive men in it along with the ball. Move
in and help and then move back to your own area
after the situation is in hand.
5. It is imperative that you talk and communicate with
your teammates, especially when you switch or need
help in your area.
6. Never take wild chances and leave your area unpro-
tected.
7. If your man shoots, he should be shooting under the
worst possible conditions. If he is not, you are at fault.
8. Always be thinking ahead about whom you are going
to block out after the shot is taken.

9. If you are undecided as to which one of two men you
should take, always take the man who is nearest the
basket.

10. In this defense, you can never let up. The pressure
must be kept on the opponents at all times.

These are the principles under which the pressing zones
operate best.

The 2-1-2 Pressing Zone

Figure 75 illustrates the basic alignment of the 2-1-2
pressing zone defense. The personnel are the same as they
are in the 2-3 pressing zone. The main point of variance is
the different area assignments of the players. X^1 and X^2
have the same assignment, but X^3 has more territory to
cover than in the 2-3 press. Figure 76 shows the different
areas of defense in the 2-1-2 pressing zone. X^4 and X^5, the
two wings of the back line, have to cover from approxi-
mately the corner on their side to the middle of the foul
lane. These are only basic limitations and will change with
each offensive move as has already been explained.

The 3-2 Pressing Zone Defense

The basic formation of the 3-2 defense can be seen in
Figure 77. This defense is strong against outside shooting
teams. X^1 is the middle man on the front row. His job is to
take any man in his area (Figure 78) and to try to prevent
any direct passes into the foul circle to the pivot man. X^3
and X^2 are the wingmen and they do not play too tightly,
but rather, out to the side of the foul circle. The wingmen
do not collapse when the ball is passed into the pivot area.
When a man moves into the pivot area, either X^4 or X^5
has to move up to help the back man. These two working

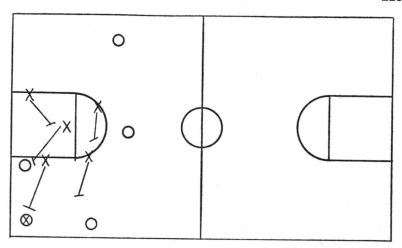

FIGURE 74. Adjusting to an Overloaded Area.

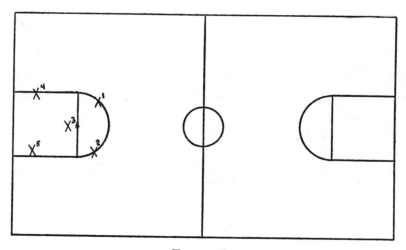

FIGURE 75.

together can make it pretty hot for a pivot man. The back
men in the 3-2 zone are X^4 and X^5. These two men move as
a unit. Because of the large area that these two players
must cover, this defense will tend to be weakest in their
areas. Their areas include from corner to corner, including

the entire baseline and the entire foul lane. Figure 79 shows an example of their movements. Usually, X^4 and X^5 can operate by one basic rule. The man nearest the ball in his area takes the ball and the remaining defensive man takes the opponent who is nearest the ball and between the ball and the basket.

One of the critical areas in the use of this particular defense is the teamwork between the back man and the wingman on the same side when they switch the dribbler. If X^2 presses his man and he dribbles toward the corner, X^5 must be there to pick him up immediately. They must be especially careful not to allow the dribbler to split between them. If this happens, an easy basket usually results.

The 1-3-1 Pressing Zone Defense

The strongest characteristic of the 1-3-1 pressing zone is its effective defense of the pivot area. It is different than most of the other defenses in that the area assignments

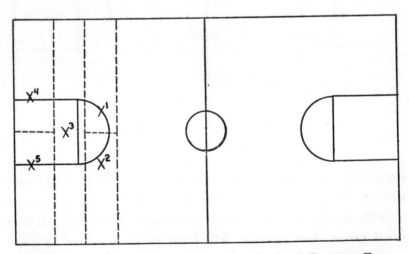

FIGURE 76. The Basic Formation for the 2-1-2 Pressing Zone.

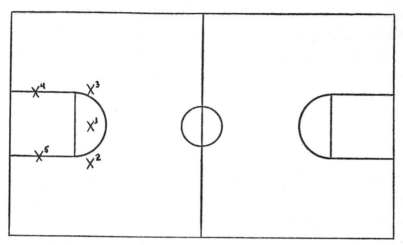

FIGURE 77. The Basic Formation for the 3-2 Pressing Zone.

utilize the personnel in a manner different from the rest of the pressing zone defenses.

Figure 80 illustrates the basic formation and the personnel changes in this defense. X^1 is the single man out front and his assignment is to prevent any outside shot near the back of the foul circle. It is also his duty to prevent any passes from going into the pivot area. A team which uses an offense that puts two men outside usually to play on either side of X^1, will have to be defensed by positioning X^1 between the two offensive men where he may reach one as quickly as the other.

X^4 and X^5 play the wing positions and you will notice that we use our pivot man and our largest forward for these positions. It is not that we need slower and taller men in these positions, rather, we need the shorter and faster men for the other positions.

X^2 is assigned the middle position. The player in this position must have the ability to diagnose plays quickly and have the fast reflexes that are required to help out in all of the surrounding areas. However, his first responsibility is to protect the pivot area.

The man who guards the entire baseline from corner to corner is X^3, the fastest forward. He moves along the baseline parallel with the ball wherever it is. Figure 81 shows the different defensive areas in this defense.

THE BOX AND ONE PRESSING ZONE

The box and one zone is, as you might suspect, used only under extreme circumstances. X^1, our best guard, is assigned one man on the opponent team and he defenses all

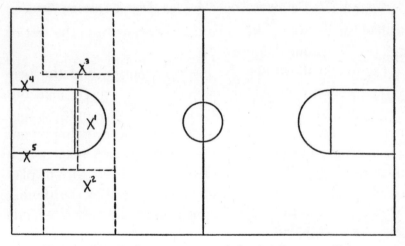

FIGURE 78. Defensive Areas of the 3-2 Pressing Zone.

over the court. This one man is usually a very high scorer that conventional defenses cannot stop. He is defensed on a man for man basis by X^1 and also picked up by a zone man when he moves into his area. This gives us a double-team situation in the high percentage shooting areas.

The other four players—X^2, X^3, X^4 and X^5—play a 2-2

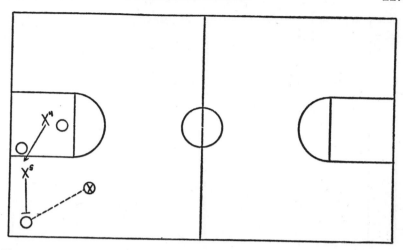

FIGURE 79. The Movements of the Back Line in the 3-2 Pressing Zone.

zone. X^2 and X^3 are the two front men and X^4 and X^5 are the two back men. These men do not press in the true sense of the word, but concentrate on preventing the opposing team from getting good shots. This defense is shown in Figures 82 and 83.

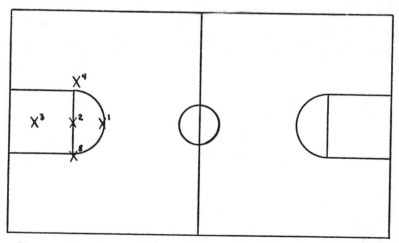

FIGURE 80. The Basic Formation of the 1-3-1 Pressing Zone.

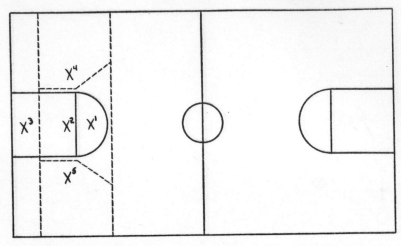

FIGURE 81. Defensive Areas of the 1-3-1 Pressing Zone.

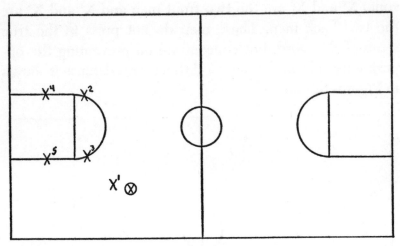

FIGURE 82. The Basic Formation of the Box and One Zone.

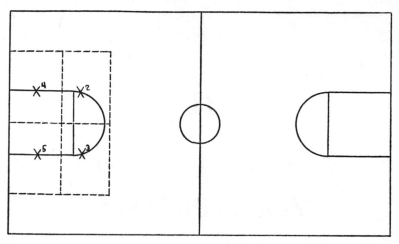

FIGURE 83. Defensive Areas of the Zone.

11

COMBATING THE ZONE PRESSES

Knowledge of how to combat the zone presses is essential for any coach even if his team employs the zone press defenses. If a team is to operate successfully against a zone press, they must use a style of play that is as fast and as aggressive as the fast break offense and the pressing defenses themselves. Movement is essential to combat the zone press. The very fact that a team must be fast and aggressive in order to combat these defenses is very difficult to the team that uses a semi-control or control ball offense and a sluggish defense, because it represents a totally different concept of basketball for them. In view of this, it is safe to assume that a team that uses an aggressive style of play has a decided advantage over a team that is not so intrepid in its style of play.

WHAT IS A WELL-ORGANIZED TEAM?

Quite often in this book, I have referred to the term "organized team". An organized team is one that knows, through the medium of advance planning and practice, exactly what to do in every situation that is likely to occur during a game. Many teams are organized to the extent of knowing what to do on offense and defense, but the better teams also take into consideration such things as: (1) taking the ball out of bounds, (2) jump ball situations, (3) foul shooting situations, and (4) changes of strategy by the opposing team. The zone presses thrive on half-organized teams.

Bringing the Ball In-Bounds

One of the first important phases of your organization is to designate one man to take the ball out of bounds every time, except for those times when the ball is to be taken out on the sides of the court. This man will usually be your slowest forward. He is the most logical man because the fastest forward should be in-bounds to cut and break for the ball. Many teams use their center to take the ball out of bounds, but we want our center to be moving down the court to set up for offense because we bring the ball up as quickly as we possibly can. The man who takes the ball out of bounds should know where each and every man is located without looking and each man on the floor should know where each of his teammates is, also. With this kind of organization, the passer will know the general area of each man and will be able to anticipate his moves to get open. This will keep team balance and prevent confusion.

When a backcourt press is giving you a very difficult time, there are several ways of getting the ball in-bounds. One is to break a guard to the man-out-of-bounds and let him literally hand the ball to the guard. The guard goes to the baseline in this maneuver so that there is no room for his defensive man between himself and the ball.

Another method consists of the two guards crossing in the middle of the floor in a moving screen. This should free one guard for receiving the pass. This maneuver is shown in Figure 84. Another simple maneuver that we use quite often to free a guard in the backcourt is the slide screen,

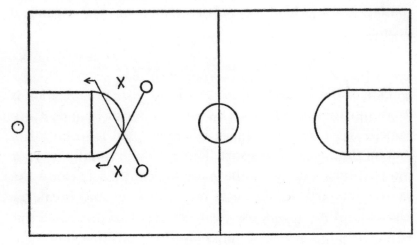

FIGURE 84. Moving Screen for the Guards.

FIGURE 85. The Slide Screen.

which is depicted in Figure 85. We work on this maneuver in practice to develop it to a high degree of speed and precision.

As a last resort, when it appears that we may not get the ball in-bounds within the required time limit, our player who is out of bounds is instructed to bounce a pass off the defensive man's leg. This will provide us with another opportunity to put the ball in play.

To be on the safe side, we always have several back-court plays in reserve to be used only when they are absolutely necessary.

Figure 86 represents an unorthodox type of maneuver that is very seldom seen in basketball today. After the opponent team has scored, O^1 quickly grabs the ball out of the basket and jumps out of bounds toward the corner. O^3 in the opposite corner near the baseline pauses a brief second and then jumps out of bounds also. O^1 passes the ball quickly to O^3 at the other end. At the same time that O^1 passes the ball to O^3, O^2 moves in and screens the man who is guarding O^1. O^1 then breaks to receive the first pass from O^3. This maneuver will usually catch the opposing team completely off guard. This is due to a very swift change of roles for two players and the defense just cannot grasp this change as quickly as the offense.

ADVANCING THE BALL UP COURT

Once the ball is passed in-bounds, regardless of which method you use, half of the battle is over. Once in bounds the man with the ball always passes to an open man. Dribbling the ball up is, by far, the most dangerous method and usually a last resort. When bringing the ball up the floor against the different types of trap defenses you should

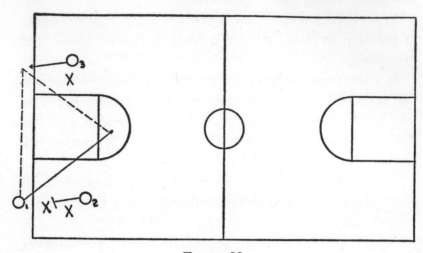

FIGURE 86.

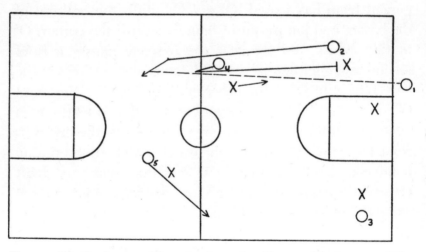

FIGURE 87. Backcourt Play Against the Press: O⁴ Screens O²'s Man and O² Breaks for the Long Pass.

be instantly aware of it when you see two men closing on the ball. When advancing the ball up the court against this type of defense, the guard should always try to advance up the middle of the court if he can. If he cannot do this,

he should move with the ball until he sees two men beginning to move in toward him. As soon as these two men
have committed themselves by a step or two, they are in
their most vulnerable position. At this split second against
the trap is the time to pass the ball.

Another good insurance against the half-court trap defense is to station a man at mid-court. This usually cuts
down on the efficiency of the trap.

One of the biggest and most frequent mistakes made by
offensive players against the zone presses is turning their
backs to the defense. When a player has the ball with his
back to the defense, he is playing right into their hands.
He cannot see any of his own teammates and he gives the
defense an opportunity to doubleteam him without his being prepared for it.

Many teams we have faced have had great difficulty in
getting the ball in from out-of-bounds and advancing it
across the mid-court line. Several of these teams have, in
an effort to bring the ball up the floor safely, brought all
five men into the backcourt area. The results were usually
that they had an even more difficult time in getting the ball
in-bounds. With so many men in the backcourt a pass
would be going to one man and another teammate would
think it was for himself. Both would go for the pass and
consequently neither usually retained possession of it.
However, with an organized team, all five men being down
the floor can be a very successful maneuver against the
zone presses. Figure 88 illustrates all five men and their
positions in the backcourt. This is actually a screening pattern designed to free a man to receive a pass from the man-
out-of-bounds.

Figure 89 shows the movements of each man in this dou-

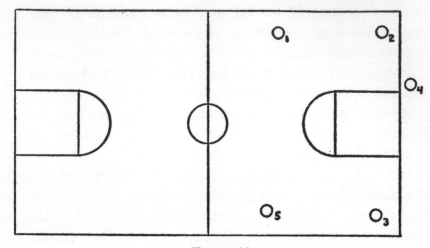

FIGURE 88.

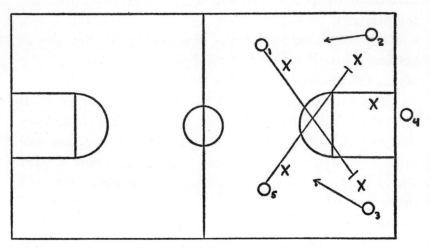

FIGURE 89. The Backcourt Double Screen.

ble screen pattern. O^5 and O^1, on a signal from the man out
of bounds (usually a slap of the ball or the call of a number), cross the floor and screen for their teammate in the
diagonal corner. O^5 screens for O^2 and O^1 screens for O^3.
O^2 and O^3 then break toward the man with the ball if they

have an opening. If they do not, they go through the very same procedure and screen for the man in the diagonal corner.

The different possibilities for bringing the ball up the court are so numerous and so varied that we do not have space to cover it in this text.

12

SPECIAL FACTORS REGARDING ZONE PRESSES

Zone presses are the types of defenses that depend upon research and change to maintain an optimum level of efficiency over a period of time. Along the same lines, there is no such thing as a team having one zone press. It is an all or nothing at all proposition. If a team has only one zone press, it does not have any press to speak of. If this were the case, you might get through one or two games before every team in the conference had your defense down on paper. Zone presses demand many variations so that you do not have to stay in several defenses for an entire game. Rather, you should have enough variations to change defenses every three or four minutes. Individually, each zone press is not a difficult pattern, but six or seven zone presses used interchangeably can be very confusing to the offensive team.

As in any defense, there are weaknesses to be reckoned with and the zone presses are certainly no exception. The zone press weaknesses are different from the rest of the defenses because you cannot know what they are and under what conditions they will appear. There are too many intangibles in these defenses to predict trouble areas before they show up.

Practice is the only place to iron out these difficulties. We always concoct an offense of our own that is designed to attack the known trouble areas and then use it against our zone defenses in practice. As soon as a mistake is made in the defense or the offense scores a basket, we immediately stop the scrimmage. Now we retrace every step of each man on offense and defense until we find the point at which our defense broke down. We point out the mistake and make the necessary correction and adjustments. After this is done, we have the offensive unit run the same play over several times to make sure that the defense has remembered the adjustment. This "grassroots" approach to defensive coaching is the most vital and essential part of the entire practice session. Without this type of treatment, the zone press will never be very successful for you and our team. It may turn out to be more confusing and chaotic than useful and effective.

As you have gathered by now, zone press defense is highly idealistic in its basic philosophy. We are constantly stressing that each man should prevent his man's receiving a pass. Of course, this will not always be possible, but we feel that it does make our team more defense conscious, and consequently we receive a greater athletic output on the court from the players.

When we experience a certain type of offense that is efficient against the zone presses and the pressing zone, we diagram and file it away. This type of evaluation helps to adjust defenses, choose the correct defenses, and create new defenses.

It is only fair to mention something about the selection of players for your team. I must say that most of our players have not been standout high school players, and in quite a number of cases, have not had the good fortune to have made high school athletic teams at all. The secret is the proper selection of personnel and hard work on the part of the player and the coach.

13

EXPERIMENTAL
ZONE PRESS

GOODRICH K. PHILLIPS, ASSISTANT COACH

"**N**ecessity is the mother of invention." The necessity for progressive change is evident in all endeavors. Progress demands more progress, and as it fills our needs, it inevitably creates or brings about new needs which must be met. Time dates everything and this demands creative thinking in order to succeed and contribute to the area which depends upon each individual in it for its maintenance.

The coach who discovers a certain defensive or offensive pattern that brings successful results is at a very critical period in his career. He has a very crucial decision to make. If he is endowed with the desire to achieve and the insight to look into the future, he will realize any system that remains unchanged will become outmoded and stagnant. The coaches who do not see this or who do not want to see it are on the pathway to mediocrity. There are many coaches who have been using the same systems for years without modifying them. Coaches must be constantly searching out new and different ways of doing things. This prevents the coach and the team from going stale. Never a year goes by that we are not experimenting with some new idea on defense or offense. If we used the same formations year after year it would not be very long before our opponents would know everything we are doing. We try to make some changes every year just for the strategic value it offers. Only recently, we have developed a new system of fast break, which will completely antiquate the three-man (man down the middle) fast break. We now operate a new and intricate five man fast break pattern.

The following experimental ideas have come about from research and the everyday associations with basketball defense. Of course, I will continue to ponder these ideas and develop them. I present them to you now so that you may have the same opportunity.

The "Seeing-Eye Dog" Press

This uniquely named press has very good potential as a primary (backcourt) defense. It is also unique in that it violates several basic fundamentals of defense. As you will see, this defense is amazingly simple, but at the same time, it will require a great deal of practice in order to coordinate it efficiently. The two variations of this defense will be referred to as 60A and 60B

60A Press Defense

Figure 90 illustrates the basic formation of the 60A "seeing-eye dog" pressing defense. Each opponent player is played on a man-to-man basis. As in nearly all of our backcourt presses, we play for the first pass from out of bounds.

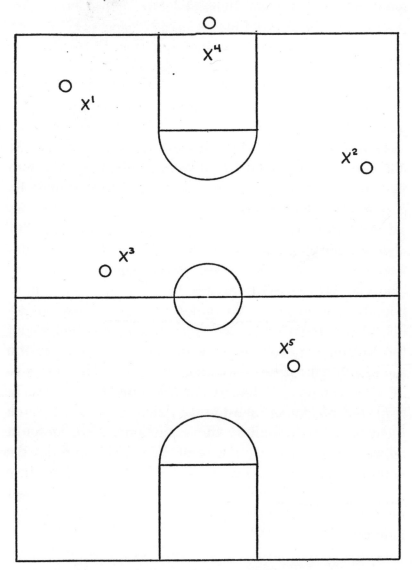

FIGURE 90. Basic Formation of the "Seeing-Eye Dog" Press.

The whole theory behind this defense is based on an unorthodox method of individual defense. During the years that I have been coaching, it has become evident that the standard man-to-man defensive practices leave something to be desired in backcourt defense. In actuality, it is very difficult to stay with a man so tightly in the backcourt that you can intercept any decent percentage of their passes from out of bounds.

At certain times in the past, we have used backcourt defenses that had two of our defensive men guarding with their backs to the ball. Reflecting back this seemed to be a more effective means of backcourt defense from the standpoint of not letting the opponent get the ball. This experimental defense employs this type of individual defense with all defensive men. Each man plays his man head-on and, if necessary, his back to the man out of bounds. The moment the opponent player steps out-of-bounds for the pass-in, our defensive men forget about the ball for the time being. Instead, they concentrate on the man to whom they have been assigned. This seems to be an easier type of defense for the individual player. In the standard type of man-to-man defense, one must watch the man and the ball at the same time. Also, he must adjust to his opponent's fakes and feints. This burdens the defensive man with several difficult tasks. Face-to-face guarding demands only one such task: stay with your man. It is advisable to stress the following points on this defense:

1. Always stay between your man and the ball.
2. Never, under any circumstances, be any further from your man than two feet.

3. If your man is extra shifty and difficult to guard, watch only his belt buckle. It cannot fake you.
4. In case of screens, be sure that the switch or slide maneuver is called quickly without losing your man.
5. Call out any possible screens in time for your teammate to react and adjust.
6. Always keep your arms at least shoulder high.
7. Do not worry about the man-out-of-bounds with the ball.
8. Try to keep your man out of the area near the passer-out-of-bounds.
9. Always be on your toes, ready to move quickly.
10. Each man must guard his man as though his very life depended upon it.

With these fundamentals in mind, you can proceed with the theory of the defense. Each man is assigned a code number, such as 1, 2, 3, 4, 5, etc. Each man on the team must know each other man's code number to the point of calling it automatically. Chapter 15 has several reaction drills listed, which will prove valuable in teaching these code numbers.

After each basket by your team, X^4 quickly picks up the man who is to throw the ball in from out-of-bounds. His duty is to completely and thoroughly harass the passer. Always be sure to obstruct his vision as much as possible. Be sure to keep the arms moving at all times. He must not throw an accurate pass or clearly see his target. This is one of the essential parts of any backcourt defense and probably the most neglected.

Each player guards his man without any concern for the ball. *His job is to stay within 12 to 24 inches of him at all times.* The center, X^5, is the only man that does not have his back to the ball. His man is usually the least prospective receiver of the first pass because of the distance involved in getting it to him.

The attitude of the passer out-of-bounds undergoes a distinct change when he sees the defense with their backs to the ball. It tends to put him at ease and give him a false sense of security. This sense of security breeds recklessness which in turn spawns mistakes. He reasons that since the defensive man is not looking, he will lob a lead pass over his head. This is logical because the defensive man cannot see or know that the pass is on its way.

Every man has a great deal of responsibility in this defense, but the way the center carries out his job determines the success or failure of it. The center, by virtue of the facts that he is up the court with all of the playing area view and does not have to defense tightly, is the "seeing-eye dog." He calls the shots. He must know every man's code number and have it instantly when it is needed. He must think and act quickly at all times.

His first duty, however, is to guard against the quick, long pass. After this danger is past, he assumes a position near his own man where he may closely observe the man trying to pass the ball in from out of bounds at the other end of the court. It is essential that the center take advantage of every tip that he can get from the passer. These little hints, plus a certain amount of intuition, save precious split seconds that mean the difference between completed pass and interception. Some of the things that the center will want to keep in mind are the following:

1. Watch the stance (foot position) of the passer.
2. A square stance usually does not signal a long pass.
3. A staggered stance permits either a long or a short pass.

4. Notice where he looks.

5. Besides watching the passer, know where each of your own players are on the court.

6. Do not anticipate your call. Be sure.

7. Do not let your own man stray away from you.

8. Move as close to mid-court as your man will allow.

9. Be prepared to advance quickly if a pass is overthrown and you can intercept it.

10. If the first pass is completed, be prepared to defend until your teammates get back.

When the center realizes where the pass is going, he must quickly call out the code number of his teammate who is guarding the intended receiver. Figure 91 illustrates the first pass being thrown to X^1's man. The center, after seeing where the ball is going, must yell, "ONE." This call must be of sufficient volume for everyone on the floor to hear it. Upon hearing his number called, X^1 now knows that the ball is in flight toward his man. His head must turn to look for the ball automatically when he hears his number. If he has correctly guarded his man, he is no more than two feet from him. This proximity should put X^1 close enough to get to the pass. If he cannot get to it, neither should the man he is guarding. If he cannot get to it, it is probably a bad pass. X^1 now has one remaining job after his number is called and that is the deflection of the ball toward mid-court. Naturally, X^1 is to intercept the ball, if he possibly can, but we are primarily interested in his deflecting the ball toward mid-court or toward the middle of the court. Many times X^1, or whoever happens to be in this situation, will have to bodily dive for the ball in order to get a hand on it for the deflection.

The other three men—X^2, X^3, and X^4—are not just guarding their men, but when they hear a number called that

is not their own, they immediately look and drop toward
the middle of the court. Here they should pick up the
deflected ball and start the fast break. These movements
are illustrated by Figure 92. With X^2, X^3 and X^4 closing
in for the ball, we should stand a good chance of retrieving
it. It is worthwhile to mention at this point that we teach
our players to fight for loose balls. Recovery of loose balls
wins many games. If a player can pick up the ball without
danger of having it stolen by the opponents, he should
do so. However, if there are several players in the same
area, the ball should be dived on so that we may at least
obtain a jump ball. X^5 is the only man who must play
cautiously after the deflection of the first pass unless he
can obtain undisputed possession of the ball.

Occasionally, there will be some doubt in the center's
mind as to where the pass is actually going. For example,
if two opponent players are very close together, either
might appear to be the intended receiver at the early stage
of the pass when the call must be made. In a situation such
as this, we have arbitrarily divided the back court into
three zones—A, B, and C. Figure 93 shows these zones.
In Figure 94, X^1 and X^2 are guarding two men that are
very close together. The center, in order to make sure that
both men will be ready, calls, "ONE A." This alerts X^1
and the call of "A" alerts anyone in the "A" zone. The
call would be just as correct if it had been, "TWO A,"
since X^2 is in the area, also.

60B Press Defense

The variation of this defense, 60B, is simply moving X^4
from guarding the man out of bounds to any place that is
appropriate for the situation. Figure 95 shows X^4 placed

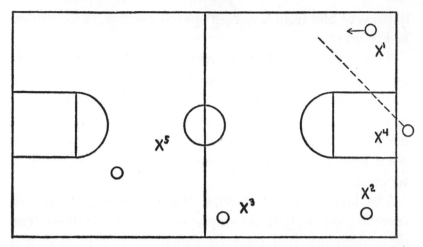

FIGURE 91. The First Pass. The Call is "ONE."

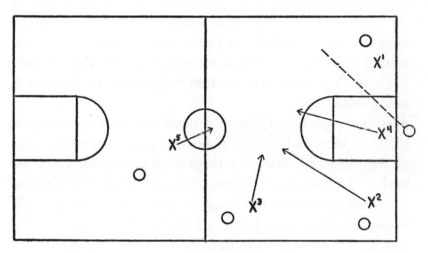

FIGURE 92. After the Call of "ONE."

near the foul mark. Here he must use his own discretion and be especially alert in not allowing any of the other men to break in for a short pass. Another situation might involve having to doubleteam an especially slippery player

to prevent him from breaking open for a pass, as illustrated
in Figure 96.

The next defense is one that we have been experimenting with to use against teams that have set offenses with
intricate plays and patterns. Its main objective is to con-
fuse the opponents and to prevent them from knowing
what type of defense we are using. If a team cannot decide
what kind of defense you are using, it cannot attack it
successfully.

The actual strategy behind this defense is the use of
several defenses that are employed at different times. The
main difficulty is a code or signalling system that will
change the team from one defense to another and back
again, smoothly and with every man being fully aware of
the change. Changing often from a zone defense into a
man for man defense and back again could be very up-
setting to a team that uses set patterns and plays mainly
because they are never certain what type of defense is
being used.

In our experimentation, we have settled on several cue
methods of signalling the defensive change. For the sake
of simplicity, we will use a drop back man-to-man defense
and a "3-2" zone as our two defenses. Code "X" denotes
a certain portion of the court. The defense automatically
changes when the ball moves into the shaded area in Figure 97. The man-to-man defense is used when the ball is
outside of the shaded area. It may be played as loosely
or as tightly as one desires. If it is played in a medium
tight fashion, it will tend to make it contrast with the zone
defense. When the ball is dribbled or passed into the
shaded area, the team automatically goes into a "3-2" zone
defense.

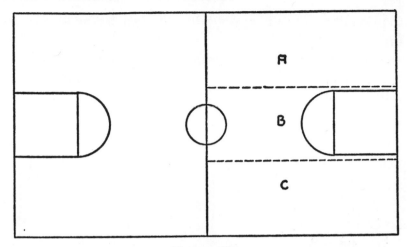

FIGURE 93.

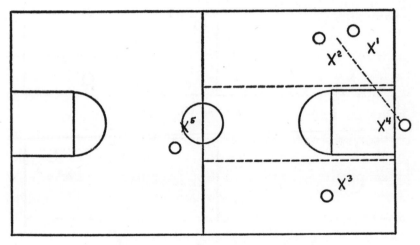

FIGURE 94. The Call is "ONE A."

Code "Y" is another zone division of the forward court which is illustrated by Figure 98. For instance, when the ball is located on side "A" of the court, the man-to-man defense is used and the "3-2" zone is employed when the ball is moved into side "B."

One good use for a changing defensive game such as this might be to contain an exceptional player on the opponent team. If that exceptional player happens to be a forward, you might go into a zone whenever he receives the ball. This should limit his ability to drive and force him to shoot the low percentage shots from outside.

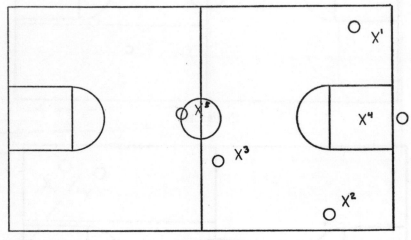

FIGURE 95.

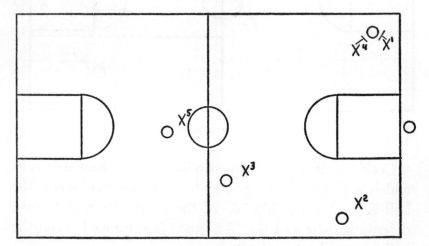

FIGURE 96.

Figures 99 through 102 illustrate court situations and the defensive adjustment for them.

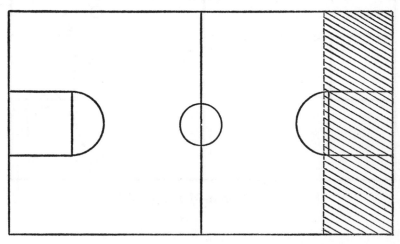

FIGURE 97. Code "X."

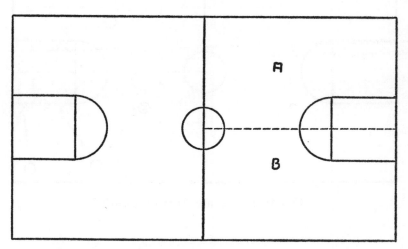

FIGURE 98. Code "Y."

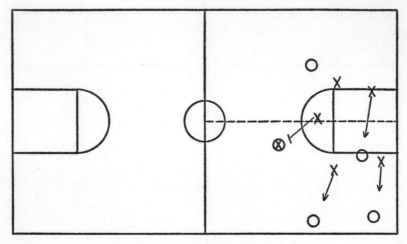

FIGURE 99. Man-to-Man Side of Court.

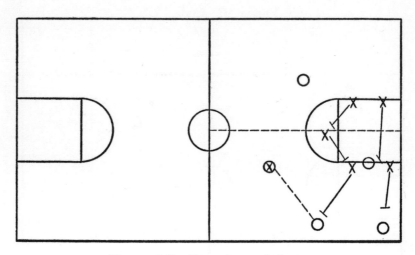

FIGURE 100. Zone Area of Court.

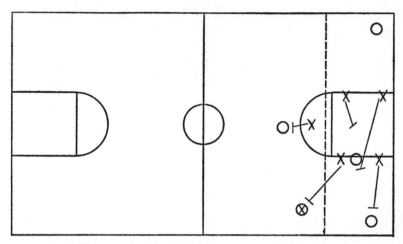

FIGURE 101. Man-to-Man Area of Court.

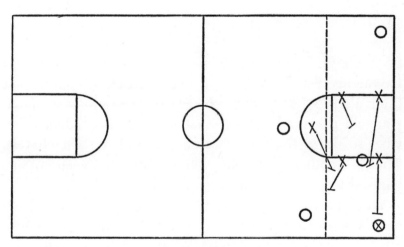

FIGURE 102. Zone Area of Court.

14

GAME STRATEGY

Game strategies are the decisions made on Saturday that are judged on Monday as right or wrong depending upon whether or not you won. This is part of basketball tradition. I suspect, however, that it is not quite as cut and dried as it has always been said to be. Game strategy is an area or a phase of basketball just as are offense and defense. Many coaches do not treat it as such; rather, they would allow those close games to be decided by Providence alone. When you find a coach who does not think about strategy until the critical moment is at hand, you will also find a team that has had no coaching on what to do in those closing moments of a tight contest. This is another fact that differentiates between an organized team and a half-organized team.

We always stress strategy to the squad, especially during the days preceding a difficult game. We have pre-season chalk talks (blackboard sessions) in which we dedicate a portion of the time to a treatment of late game strategy. Some of the points that we stress in these sessions are as follows:

1. When only a few seconds remain in the game and a basket is needed, throw the ball in-bounds as near

to mid-court as possible and then obtain a timeout. After the timeout, you will be close enough to make one pass-in and get a shot.

2. If we have a foul-shot situation and are behind by three points, we shoot to make the first shot. If the shot is missed, we shoot to miss the second shot and rebound it and possibly get a three-point play. If we make the first shot, instead of missing it, call time out. During the timeout we will insert our largest combination of players to give us an edge on the forthcoming rebound. We miss the second shot deliberately and play for the tip or the rebound.

3. Never allow a man dribbling for a layup to make it a three-point play. Try to bother him, but do not foul.

4. Do not call timeouts unless they are absolutely necessary.

5. Never lose your temper in a game and if you notice one of your teammates getting "steamed" up, try to calm him down. An angry ball player is useless and is liable to do great harm to a team effort.

6. Never argue or talk to the officials. This is the coach's job. When a player draws a technical foul, he sits on the bench for the rest of the game. These are inexcusable on the part of the player.

7. If you have four fouls against you, do not slack up on defense. Most men are much better off with five fouls than they are with four. You should play as if you had only one foul.

8. If a player on the opposing team has four fouls on him, we want to work in his area. If we find that he is more concerned with remaining in the game than he is with his defense, it is all the better for us.

9. Do not try to conceal an injury from the coach. It will only harm you and the team.

10. If we obtain possession of the ball with as little as one minute to go before the end of first half, we control it and take a sure shot or the last shot, whichever presents itself first.

Some of the things that contribute to good game strategy are: (1) keeping ahead of the rules and their changes from year to year, and (2) creating an awareness on the part of the player as to the importance of this strategy.

TIMEOUTS

In regard to time out, I tend to be very conservative. In many of our games we do not make use of a single timeout. We play a running game and everything depends upon keeping the pressure on the opponent team. When we call a timeout, we are helping them to rest and recover. In the event of a close game, the timeout is the only compensating mechanism that you have besides your bench strength. We always have a manager keep count of our timeouts so that we do not exceed our limit. Generally, most of our timeouts are called from the bench.

SIGNALS

Our defenses are so many, with each defense having several variations, we have found it necessary to code them for quick and understandable use. Generally, we will have two series which are the two basic defenses, man-to-man and zone. The 50 series represents a man-to-man defense and the 20 series represents the zone press defenses. The second digit in the 50 or 20 series denotes the specific defense such as the 3-2, 2-3, or the 2-1-2. For example, 24 would instantly tell you that it is a zone press, "2," and the digit "4" might indicate a 2-1-2 alignment on the court. All of our defenses are employed at different positions on the court and so to indicate the location of these defenses, we add a letter such as "A" or "B." The letter "A" indicates a full-court press, "B" indicates a three-quarter court press, "C" represents a half-court defense, and "D" is indicative of the drop back defense. Therefore, 24A would represent a full-court 2-1-2 zone press. On the full court defenses, we sometimes put a defensive man on the man-out-of-bounds. To indicate this situation in our code, we add a plus sign to the code number.

Our defenses will rattle some opponents and force them to call timeout in order to adjust. Everytime the opponents call a timeout we change our defense. This way they experience great difficulty in adjusting to the defenses and it also forces them to use up their allotted timeouts much more quickly than they ordinarily would.

We like to put the pressure on the younger and less experienced players. If a player is going to be "rattled," most certainly the zone presses will be more than sufficient to do it. It has been my experience that the players themselves can spot a player of this type much quicker than the coach. We rely on the judgment of our boys in regard to this matter.

THE LAST MINUTE RUSH

This is one of the most familiar scenes in basketball. For the team that is losing the last minutes of a basketball game demands an increased effort on their part in order to win. Many teams start this last minute rush and most usually fall short. If a "rush" is to begin, it should begin no later than five minutes before the end of the game and it is my belief that there should be no difference in the way you play the game regardless of the time that remains, especially when your team is losing. When we are behind, the team should be going full tilt and the only reason to

slow down would be for the game to end. We do everything that we can to prevent our team from ever coasting
or taking it easy. We want them to know nothing but 100
per cent basketball. When we are beating a team badly,
we do not allow our first unit to coast. We take them out
of the game and substitute our second unit who will go
full tilt. We substitute for the following reasons:

1. When a player is in foul trouble.
2. When a player is doing a poor defensive job.
3. When the team is handily beating the opponents.
4. We take out any player who argues with an official
   or who draws a technical foul.
5. In a close game when an opponent has a foul shot coming, during a crucial part of the game, we will usually substitute in order to apply a bit more pressure
   to him.
6. We substitute occasionally for the purpose of changing
   the defense.

15

INDEX OF OFFENSIVE
AND DEFENSIVE DRILLS

Offensive and defensive basketball can be only as good as the drills that break each down into component parts for specialized attention.

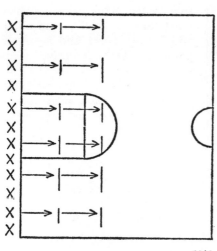

DRILL 1: Line up the squad along the baseline and have them count off in twos. On the whistle, the number ones move out as fast as they can and on the next whistle, they stop in their tracks. Good defensive stance should be stressed throughout this entire drill. When everyone is stopped, call attention to the foot position of every man and stress that bent-knee position.

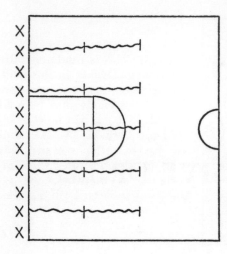

Drill 2: This drill involves the same principles as Drill 1, except that we use a ball and the boys dribble instead of run. On the whistle, the ones dribble straight ahead until the next whistle. On the next whistle, every man stops and dribbles in place. Again, stress position. This procdure is repeated for the entire length of the court. We make the players use the left and right hands alternately in separate drills.

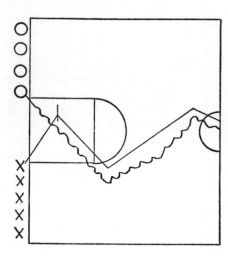

Drill 3: This one-on-one drill is the basis of our whole defensive system. One offensive man must take the ball to the other end of the court and score, if possible. The defensive man must stop him and take the ball away from him, if possible. At the far end each man comes back up the floor and gets in the opposite line.

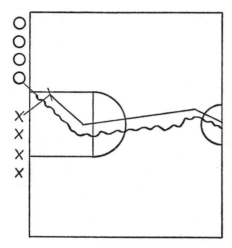

DRILL 4: This is fundamentally the same as Drill 3. In this drill, the defensive man can use only his feet. His hands must be held behind his back. He must keep his body between his man and the basket. After we use this drill to demonstrate the importance of footwork, we go back and work on Drill 3 again.

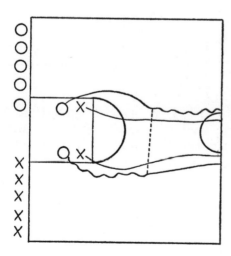

DRILL 5: This is a two-on-two drill. Two offensive and defensive players oppose each other the length of the floor. The defense must try to steal the ball but still prevent their defensive man from breaking away. You may also vary this drill by having the defensive men hold their hands behind their back.

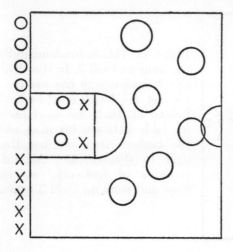

DRILL 6: This drill is designed to keep the defensive man alert for screens. Several chairs are placed on the court and moved in to different positions after the defensive man has turned to face his man. The defensive men should call out screens for each other and they should also be feeling with an extended arm for the screens so as to avoid them.

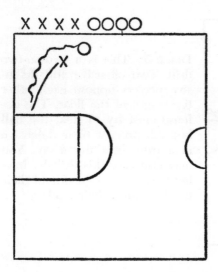

DRILL 7: This is worked the same way as our regular one-on-one drill except that it is off the side.

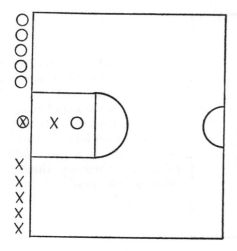

DRILL 8: This drill is to train the defensive man to play the offensive man or potential pass receiver in such a tight manner that he cannot receive the pass from the passer out of bounds.

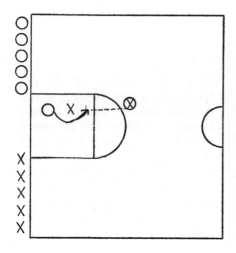

DRILL 9: We use this drill early in the season. It drills the individual on the fundamentals of faking, and cutting to receive the ball in the pivot area. A manager or player stands out behind the foul circle and makes the pass-in. The defensive man tries to intercept or deflect the pass.

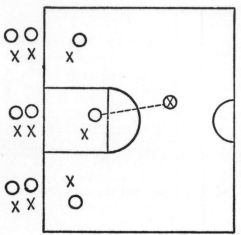

DRILL 10: This drill utilizes the two forwards and the center and their defensive men. After the pass-in from the man behind the circle, the center shoots and the defensive men block out and rebound. This is a good drill to teach the block-out since it is done at full speed.

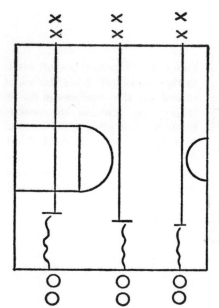

DRILL 11: In this drill, the offensive men start moving across the floor quickly. As soon as they begin to dribble, the defensive man has to move up fast and stop the man while maintaining good defensive position. This fundamental of mastering a quick controlled stop will be essential for the different trap defenses.

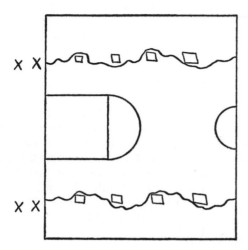

DRILL 12: This is a drill that is designed to promote good dribbling with both hands. A man dribbles at full speed around chairs or other obstacles placed on the floor. The player changes hands on each chair. For example, if he goes around the first chair with his right hand, he will use his left to dribble around the next obstacle.

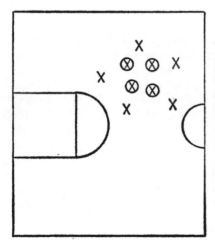

DRILL 13: This is a ball handling drill. The players form two circles, one inside the other. The outside circles will move clockwise and the inside circle, counter-clockwise, or vice versa. While they are moving, they pass the ball from one circle to the other. As many as three or four balls may be used at one time.

DRILL 14: We put our pivot men and forwards through this drill every day. The man with the ball assumes a position in front or to the side of the basket. Then the three defensive men swarm around him on a signal from a whistle and he has to put the ball in the basket. This gets a boy used to being double-teamed on offensive rebounds and teaches what to do with the ball in these situations.

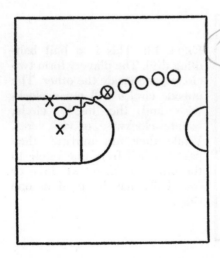

DRILL 15: This drill is to teach our men to drive. It is to acquaint them under simulated game conditions, with the opposition they will have to contend with. The man with the ball dribbles and splits the two defensive men with a drive and attempts to make the basket. The two defensive men allow themselves to be split, but try to block the ball without fouling.

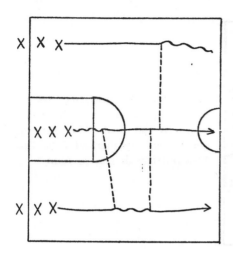

DRILL 16: This is the drill used for sharpening up the three-man fast break. The middle man passes to one side, etc. We also will run this drill without a single dribble and often by tipping the ball from man to man without catching it.

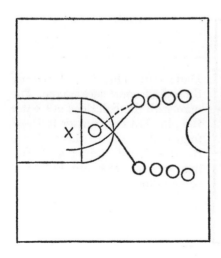

DRILL 17: The two lines of players behind the circles work the ball around and pass in to the pivot man who breaks for the pass. They break on the opposite sides of the pivot man while he attempts to pass off to one of them.

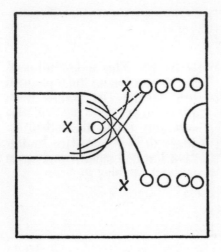

DRILL 18: We add two defensive men to increase the difficulty of the drill. The moving screen must be combated by the two outside defensive men.

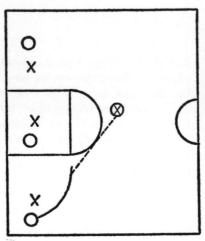

DRILL 19: This is a three-on-three half court scrimmage. The man with the ball does not enter the play but only passes to those men that break. In this drill we stress defense, sliding and calling screens, blocking out, and rebounding.

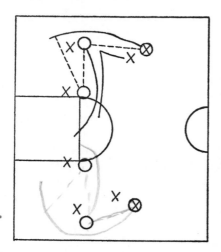

DRILL 20: This guard around drill familiarizes the players with the different options that are available. We work it on both sides of the foul circle in order to accommodate more players at one time.

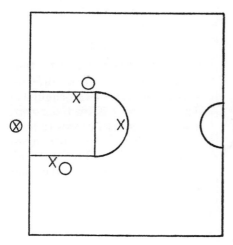

DRILL 21: This drill simulates the actual game condition of a backcourt press with a floater. The defense attempts to intercept the pass. The passer-out-of-bounds has only five seconds to get the ball into play.

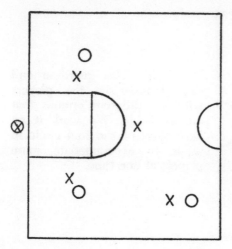

DRILL 22: This drill is identical to the one above except an additional offensive and defensive man has been added. This simulates still another backcourt situation.

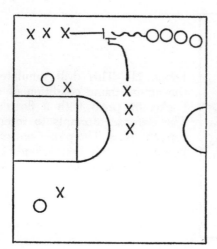

DRILL 23: Practice on the fundamentals of the trap defense is essential. This drill simulates the side trap. It is for those men who actually trap in this type of defense. The offensive man should try to get off a good pass if possible to the offensive man on the far side.

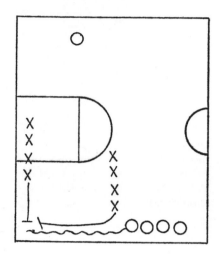

DRILL 24: This drill simulates the corner trap that is found in several of our defenses. The pass should be thrown to the offensive man on the far side.

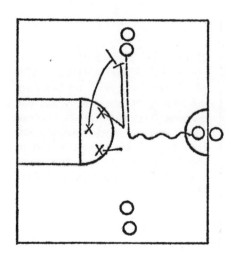

DRILL 25: This drill is designed to simulate that vital segment of the 2-1-2 zone press. This as you can see is also a trap. It should teach these front men to act as a single unit.

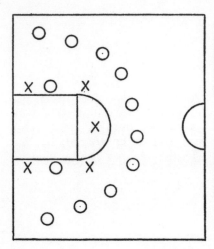

DRILL 26: This drill teaches the shifts and areas of our 3-2 zone press. We place seven to nine men around the outside of the foul circle and allow them to work the ball around for a good shot. The outside men cannot move inside, but they may pass in to the two pivot men inside. We tell our defense that they should not allow a single shot.

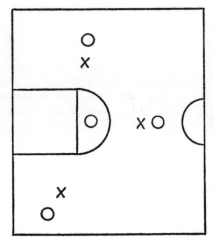

DRILL 27: This drill is a half-court offensive exercise. The pivot man does nothing but pass off and does not enter into the offense. The players should use their screens and set-ups that they have been taught to get to the basket or to get the good shot. This is also a good defensive drill.

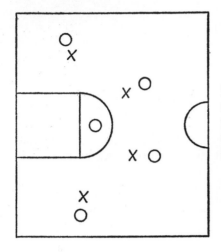

DRILL 28: This is a drill similar to the one above with the exception of the addition of one more offensive man. The center remains restricted in this drill.

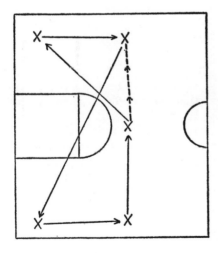

DRILL 29: A figure eight passing and cutting drill that we use to sharpen our pass and cut series is also useful in the development of general fundamentals. After we run it unopposed for a few minutes we add five defensive men.

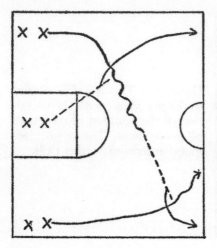

DRILL 30: This is a figure eight fast break drill that is executed down the entire length of the court. The passer cuts behind the man to whom he passes.

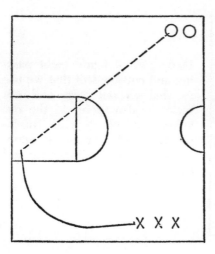

DRILL 31: This is a passing drill that we use to sharpen up our baseball passing. We like the pass to be right at fingertip height so that the man driving in does not have to break stride but can lay it in while in the air.

16

SPECIALIZED
TRAINING TECHNIQUES

Coaching zone press defensive basketball demands much more attention to the utilization of different and specialized techniques. Creating challenging and interesting methods of attacking fundamental weaknesses is essential. If your drills are not interesting and motivational, the players will not learn as much as they need to. For instance, each boy on the team is required to shoot fifty foul shots each day of the week (except Sunday) during season and the high total for the week will get a milkshake or something similar. With the weekly results being posted on the bulletin board outside of the gymnasium, the boys are all careful to take their time so that they may enter as good a score as possible. This ego appeal usually works.

VISUAL AIDS

We film some of our home games every year and use them as teaching aids for the zone press defenses. The most valuable films that we have are those that show offenses that went well against the defenses. We then follow this up with blackboard sessions on how these defenses are to be adjusted in order to cope with this particular type of offense.

In our dressing room we always have several "slogans" hung on the walls for the purpose of subliminally stimulating the players. In addition to these, we put up signs that pertain to the next game that we are to play. This tends to keep the players in the proper frame of mind throughout the days prior to the next game.

On the walls at eye level, we post different types of charts (from sporting goods concerns) that illustrate good form in many of the fundamental skills that are associated with basketball. It has already been mentioned in this book about the charts and graphs that we keep on each individual player. I cannot stress their importance too much.

A POINT SYSTEM

A point system is the scoring system that we use in one of our motivational games and even in our regular season games. A team consists of any number of players from one to five. It is a basketball game played on a half court. The only difference between it and actual basketball is the system of scoring points. The defense may score as many or more points as the offense and never have the ball. The following scoring system is used:

Basket . . . . one point
Missed shot . . . . minus one point
Block shot . . . . two points
Offensive rebound . . . . one point
Defensive rebound . . . . one point
Steal . . . . one point

If defensive man causes an
   offensive man to miss the
   entire basket on a shot . . one point
Bad pass .... minus one point
Foul .... minus one point
Layup .... minus two points for defense

The offense keeps control of the ball as long as they can score. To provide a little more motivation, the losing team must run as many laps as they are deficient in points. This prevents any loafing.

HANDBALL

One of the games that we insist our players participate in is handball, which develops many desirable things in the individual. They are as follows:

1. Hand-eye coordination
2. Agility
3. Calf and thigh muscles
4. Endurance
5. Ambidexterity
6. Reflexes
7. Coordination
8. Correct defensive position
9. Kinesthetic sense
10. General physical condition

We have the boys play the game in several different ways. One way is to hit the ball alternately with the left and right hands. Another way is to play an entire game with the left hand or the right hand only. This game is very popular with our boys since it breaks the monotony of everyday drills. It is good diversion and it also promotes those things that are essential in basketball. Handball is an especially good post-season and pre-season sport. I personally believe handball to be the most beneficial of the off-season activities.

WEIGHTS AND APPARATUS

Weights should play an active part in a specialized conditioning program. We are interested in building special areas of the body rather than a general physical program.

Naturally, the most important area of the body for basketball is the legs. The legs of a basketball player must be subjected to a physical building program to develop and promote strength, resiliency, and endurance, in the calf and thigh mucles. These areas are mainly responsible for an individual's jumping ability. Their level of condition must be at such a high peak that they will not tire enough to cut down the efficiency in the final stages of a game. Their condition should be such that another quarter could be played without any adverse effect upon the individual player.

To condition the legs with weights we use several exercises that all accomplish the same end results: (1) Have several two-by-four pieces of lumber about three feet in length and keep them in the training or dressing rooms. With the two-by-four on the floor, spread the feet to a comfortable stance, place the toes of each foot upon the edge of the two-by-four and lift your heels up off the floor so that you are actually standing on your toes. The lift and drop should be executed at a medium speed and the latter, possibly, at a slower speed. We insist that each of our players spend at least five or ten minutes on this exercise each day. (2) We repeat the exercise that was just described, except that the player places a barbell of about twenty pounds in weight upon his shoulder. (3) In practice, we use the "duck walk" with which every coach is familiar. (4) Running up steps on the toes is also a very good exercise for strengthening of the legs.

We use several different types of apparatus in our specialized exercise department. Among these are some that are overlooked by many coaches because of their simplicity.

One of these is the common jumping rope. We buy clothesline, make wooden handles, and manufacture our own. Pre-season and early season practice are good times to pass these out to the boys who need work on them. Jumping rope is especially good for those young, awkward, big boys. When we have a big man who gets his feet tangled together, we always prescribe fifteen or twenty minutes a day on the jumping rope. He will begin with simple maneuvers and progress to others in order of difficulty. The skipping with both feet together and then one foot at a time are typical simple maneuvers.

To strengthen wrists and hands, we use a rubber ball and a weight on the end of a rope. The rubber ball is merely carried around in the palm of the hand and gripped from time-to-time. This exercise is beneficial, but we use the weight method predominantly now. Tie a ten-pound weight to the end of a three-and-a-half to four-foot length of sash cord and attach the other end of the rope to a wooden handle. The player grabs the wooden handle with both hands (one on each side of the rope) and begins to wind the sash cord upon the wooden handle. He winds the weight up to the handle and then lowers it in the same fashion. The entire operation takes place at arm's length.

In practice, we work on the wrists by dribbling a basketball against a wall at eye-level, making sure to keep it from bounding further than ten or twelve inches from the wall. This is also a very good finger and wrist exercise.

Many of our drills are developed due to the necessity for them. At one time we discovered that our boys were losing many of the rebounds that they got their hands on because of the roughness of the opponents. This unaccustomed roughness was jostling the ball from their hands before they had full control of it. Our players were not accustomed to the rough play under the boards. In order to condition our boys to this type of play, we rigged up two fifty pound upright blocking bags and hung them from the ceiling on ropes, one on each side of the basket. We put a manager or a player on each of the bags. Then each boy took his turn rebounding a ball that was thrown up against the board. Each person attending a blocking bag has to pull it back from its resting position about four or five feet. As the rebounder goes up for the ball, the attendants release the bags so that they both swing into the rebounder. The blow from both sides should be synchronized to hit at the same time that the ball is engaged by the fingers. The bags give him a much rougher time than any two opponents could without fouling him. After drilling on this for a period of time, we were not losing nearly as many balls because of roughness. This unique drill also caught the fancy of the boys and they actually looked forward to it. It offered a laugh or two for them during practice, as you might well imagine.

Our average practice will last about two and one-half hours. We place emphasis on fundamentals throughout the season. Each practice is planned each morning and every minute to be spent on the floor is accounted for. There should not be one minute of practice that is not scheduled to some activity. In practice, it will be impossible to follow this plan to the minute, but we follow it as closely as we

PLATE 7. *Three Players Engaging in a Tipping Drill.*

PLATE 8. *A Good Tipping Drill.* (Note that only finger-tips are on the ball.)

PLATE 9. *This Ball Was a Rebound; Now It's a Basket.*

possibly can. A typical practice plan is shown in Figure 103.

3:00—Warm up (Individual)
3:05—Shooting practice
3:15—Group exercises—boxer shuffle and jumps
3:30—One on one
3:40—Two on two
3:50—Three on three
4:00—Four on four
4:10—Five on five
4:20—Offense and fast-break drills
4:35—Foul shooting
4:40—Half-court scrimmage (defense)
4:55—Full-court scrimmage (defense)
5:10—Half-court scrimmage (offense)
5:20—Full-court scrimmage
5:30—Showers

FIGURE 103. Practice Plan.

17

MEDICAL ASPECTS OF CONDITIONING AND ATHLETIC INJURIES

C. W. STALLARD, JR., M.D

The approach to conditioning of athletes, both physical and psychological, can, and should be, both traditional and scientific. It is the coach's desire to bring his players to a point of maximum physical readiness, with peculiar emphasis on the specific requirements of the game played and the style in which he coaches. After reaching this point, he then desires to maintain them at an optimum level.

Psychological conditioning toward athletics and competitive sports is no less important than physical readiness, but we will dismiss the former as being entirely within the scope of the coaching staff; rarely will they need assistance in managing it.

Basketball is intensively played over a predetermined length of time in a school year. Basketball "season" has definite limits in beginning and ending. It goes without saying that physical conditioning should not be begun, realized, maintained, and discontinued over any time segment, but should be continued, at least in moderation the whole year round. However, blocking, tackling, distance-running and weight-lifting exercises are specifically designed for the sports to which they appertain, whereas basketball also has its differentiated exercise program, with specialized objectives in mind. We attempt to build upon a sound body in already good condition, and especially augment certain agilities, endurances and strengths which may not be so necessary elsewhere.

Conditioning should have begun, on the athlete's own initiative or at the coach's direction, prior to a first practice period. A gradually intensifying program of training can then be brought to a peak before the first varsity game.

Maintenance of condition, once it is reached, is obtained by continued exercises, practice sessions, maintenance of health, and the treatment of injuries and illnesses. We will restrict further discussion in this chapter to the latter two of these.

MAINTENANCE OF HEALTH

After an initial physical examination, details of medical history are investigated, along with more precise evaluation of any discovered physical defect or weakness. We have on occasion carried this to some lengths, including electrocardiograms, detailed blood studies and radiographs of chest, previously injured joints and extremities, and so forth, but usually the physical examination is supplemented only by an initial urinalysis.

The coaching staff is never expected to make the final decision as to whether or not an athlete may play. We have, however, attempted to supply enough diagnostic and prognostic information to allow his desire to influence this decision, which is made only after discussion of the physical and psychological aspects of the athlete's condition with the continuation of athletics or competition in mind.

We attempt to exercise moderate control over an athlete's schedule. Regular hours of rest and regular meals of balanced dietary needs are assured by control of on-campus athletes, less so by advice to those who live off-campus. Multiple therapeutic vitamins are dispensed to all squad members. Salt tablets are given after, but not before, drills and practice sessions. Attention is paid to weight factors—this must be geared to an optimum achievement for each individual, and factors such as growth, endocrine characteristics, body habits, predispositions to certain diseases or injuries, personal habits, and the distance lying between the initial condition and the optimum level, must be considered. Thus an overweight athlete may be put on a rigid diet and exercise program to lose ten pounds—but 30-40 pounds of weight loss may be more difficult to achieve, should take longer, and should be more carefully managed. We do prefer our basketball players to be slightly underweight by older standards; this, however, probably represents optimum health for almost all active individuals. Records of physical condition should be kept throughout the season including weight, progress toward optimum achievement, history of intercurrent illnesses, injuries, and psychological status (probably best expressed as attitude).

Treating Athletes' Illnesses

The most vigorous muscular health probably does not increase immunologic resistance to disease, so infectious illnesses of varying degrees of severity do occur. All athletes should be immunized against typhoid, diphtheria, tetanus, smallpox, poliomyelitis and influenza, provided sensitivity to vaccines does not prohibit their use. We also have given adenovirus or "cold virus" vaccines with unevaluated results.

Developing illnesses are seen promptly and treatment begun by the physician in charge. Since, in many instances, this may be a stranger who has not seen the athlete before, as on trips, a written report should be furnished to the coach so that the team physician may be made familiar with details of diagnosis and treatment.

The most frequent illnesses seem to be those of the respiratory tract, and with the exception of streptococcic tonsillitis or sore throat, most of these are of viral origin. In many instances they are not severe enough to interrupt athletic participation, but even mild illnesses prolonged may cause serious deterioration in ability to perform, and may represent menace to continuing health. So we consider that even a "slight cold" deserves the attention of the school or team physician.

Medications for these respiratory ailments include salicylates, antihistamine compounds and vasoconstrictor or expectorant drugs. Most of these will have little immediate effect on performance, and no permanent effect beyond the discontinuation of their dosage. Antihistamines may affect some individuals adversely; however, there is a wide variance in the effect of different types of this drug, and considerable variance in the individual's response. These possible side effects should be known by the coach, and athletes should be instructed not to take the widely advertised "cold remedies" without supervision; nor should they be empirically prescribed by the coaching staff.

If antibiotic drugs have been employed in the treatment of illness, it is a good general rule that the athlete should refrain from practice and competition until recovery from an illness which requires antibiotic treatment.

Since the scope of this chapter is limited to information of use to coaches, another rule regarding the illness of athletes should be followed: if the athlete's performance is obviously sub-par, the coach should get his team physician's advice, as in many cases desire and the emotional content so necessary to sustained athletic output, may cause him to avoid mention of symptoms he fears may cost him his position on the team, or his progress toward a varsity spot. Suffice to say, however, that hypochondriasis is well known among athletes as a compensating mechanism for their self-adjudged failures. Again, the physician may be necessary to make this distinction.

Major illnesses, of course, may mean the loss of an athlete for an entire season; indeed, it may preclude further participation, no matter what the athlete's desire. In this instance the coach must exercise tolerance, sympathy and understanding, as well as discretion.

Injuries are an annually recurring plague, which may cause major disruptions in a coach's program. In basketball, this is particularly so, and more particularly so in fast-moving, high scoring offensive play and pressing zone and individual-responsibility defense patterns, as the sub-par performance of a single individual may force the type of play into a pattern which falls considerably short of the desired over-all performance. Prompt evaluation of injuries and communication of prognosis of recovery is essential information to the coach. We try to provide this as quickly as possible, therefore almost all injuries are x-rayed, and protective bandaging applied immediately.

PREVENTION OF INJURIES

Injury prevention is within the scope of a conditioning program—the better-conditioned athlete in general suffers less from injury. Overstress may predispose to injury and the coach should be aware of the physical limits of his players, as he attempts to extend these very limits. Again, consultation with the team physician may help him make these evaluations.

Although occasional fractures occur, the majority of injuries seen in basketball players are muscular and ligamentous, usually involve joints and mainly the ankles, knees and fingers, in that order of frequency. They consist of sprains, strains, and ligamentous tears of greater or lesser severity. Although the training and coaching staff should not diagnose these injuries, their corrective and supportive treatment may fall within the scope of their program.

Ankles, being most frequently injured, are routinely protected by two pair of socks, outside of which nonelastic ankle wraps are used. These are usually simple figure-of-eight wrappings. If however, an ankle has been previously injured, it becomes suspected of weakness, and an adhesive wrap is always applied before any practice session or game. This varies slightly according to the configuration of the foot, but is basically a basket weave left open on the dorsum of the foot, overlaid with heel locks and finally reinforced with an overlying figure of eight. Properly applied over cotton, with the skin prepared with a benzoinated compound, this is both actually and psychologically effective. This is also the treatment for an acute strain or sprain, although it is then made heavier and more restrictive to the motion of the ankle joint.

Similar strappings are applied for strains of the plantar arch. The longitudinal arch may be strained in the rapid floor movement and sudden stops and starts required in the aggressive style of basketball. The arch may be supported by duplicating its major tendon components with applied adhesive strips, these being extended into the distal portion of the leg and firmly anchored. These adhesive strips are usually incorporated in the routine ankle supportive wrap.

In some instances, when ligamentous tears are not complete, healing and re-establishment of the integrity of the joint, may be expected; however, in others, surgical repair of the ligaments is the only curative mechanism. In these latter instances, the coaching staff will not usually be involved in corrective treatment; the entire program will be supervised by the physician. Severe injuries to the ankle joint are made most comfortable by the use of molded plaster splints extending from the toes to the midcalf, left open in front, and anchored in place by gauze bandage. Circular casting of the foot is not done unless bone injury is also present.

Shin Splints: this condition probably represents small periosteal tears at the long origin of the peroneal muscles and the long extensor muscles of the foot. These arise from the triangular (in cross section) anterior surfaces of the tibia. The resultant inflammatory process includes both pain and swelling. The use of analgesic ointments, protective sponging and wrapping probably contributes to comfort only, as the line of force causing these periosteal tears is almost parallel to the tibia. The careful use of ultra-sound, heat in the form of hydrotherapy, infrared with wet towels applied, and the oral use of chymotrypsin (orenzyme tablets, varidase buccal tablets) and related compounds, may hasten the resolution of inflammation. Some rest of the affected parts must be included, practice must be slowed or actually discontinued. Recurrence may or may not occur, but usually does not if the original inflammatory process is allowed to subside completely, and is not aggravated by further minor injuries.

Knee injuries, though less frequent, are more severe. They include sprains, strains, more critical ligamentous injuries, but also include injuries to the menisci or semilunar cartilages. The knee is more apt to show effusion into the joint capsule or the bursae about the patella. Knee injuries on the whole are more severe, take longer to heal, and are more likely to result in permanent joint derangement. While adhesive bandages are employed, we always recommend the use of a knee brace with metal side pieces. These should be of leather, laced, rather than of elastic, although the latter may suffice. It is wise to remember that an injured knee may cause the athlete painful disability for the rest of his life.

Finger injuries are frequent, but usually represent more minor injury, as the finger and hand structure has much greater mobility, and this mobility extends in several planes of motion. The usual "stoved joint" is an actual hemorrhage into the joint, with resultant swelling of the soft tissues about the joint. Even these are routinely x-rayed and properly immobilized by adhesive splinting until recovery is assured.

Severe bruises occur in most any muscles, as contact

does occur in basketball. Minor bruises represent only edema of muscles without separation of muscle fibers, and will respond to heat, massage, analgesic dressings and active use—indeed active use, though painful, will probably resolve them without further attention. More severe contusions represent bleeding into the muscle tissue and separation of its fibers—in this case active use cannot hasten the body's removal of blood clots. These are treated with ultrasound, restrictive, protective and analgesic dressings, and frequently the use of trypsin by intramuscular injection with or without infiltrating the actual hematoma with hyaluronidase.

In general, joint capsules and ligaments, bursae around joints, and trigger pain, points of muscular spasm may be injected with cortisone analogues, after it has become apparent that the inflammatory process will be prolonged.

Any acute strain, sprain or bruise should at first be treated with the objective of minimizing tissue swelling. This may be due to the escape of tissue fluids, causing a pale swelling, or actual bleeding of greater or lesser extent. Once fracture has been eliminated as a diagnostic possibility, the following program of treatment should be carried out: the ankle or other joint or extremity should be included in a compressive dressing. This may be applied with sponge rubber pads overlaid by elastic bandage. Care should be exercised that the bandage does not occlude arterial circulation (tourniquet effect). The part should then be elevated and ice packs applied over the bandage for the first 18-24 hours. Actually, in some training departments, such a compressive bandage may be applied and the part immersed in ice water for short lengths of time. A surprising amount of swelling may be eliminated by this method. After 24 hours, heat may be substituted for cold, and the compressive bandage replaced by a supportive wrap.

The use of heat on an acute injury will increase swelling, and is not advised.

Aspiration of blood from major joints (not fingers) should be performed as quickly as hemarthrosis is diagnosed. Also blood should be removed from bursae around joints. Large intramuscular clots should also be aspirated through large caliber needles, and every effort made to restore the muscle to its previous contour quickly, as blood may represent the locus for extensive scar formations, leading to calcium deposit and rarely to actual formation of bone plates within the muscle.

Facial and head injuries occur with sufficient frequency to deserve mention. Fracture of the skull and facial bones must be suspected and looked for. Fractures of the cheekbone, or zygomatic arch, and the nasal bones are perhaps the most frequently seen. These deserve professional attention, frequently that of a specialist in diseases of the nose and throat. Even "bloody noses" which cause little disability should be x-rayed as soon as feasible. Concussion resulting in unconsciousness must deserve a period of two-to-three-days' observation at relative inactivity, and persistence of neurological symptoms demands more extensive consultation, with subdural clot in mind, even though fractures do not exist.

Eye injuries are common and usually minor, although contusion of the orbit or of the eyeball itself may occur, the more frequently seen occurrence is the "finger stuck in my eye." Lacerations and abrasions of the conjunctiva and particularly the cornea must be diagnosed quickly. This may be done with relative safety by the coach, in the absence of professional help. A small plastic bottle containing 1/4 per cent pontocaine hydrochloride is carried in the first aid kit, also a bottle of 1 per cent fluorescein in a sterile buffered eye solution, and an eye irrigator containing sterile buffered saline solution. The eye may be quickly anesthetized with 3-4 drops of pontocaine and stained with a single drop of fluorescein. A corneal abrasion or laceration is easily visualized as a glowing greenish yellow defect in the transparency of the corneal membrane. If present, a physician should be promptly consulted, as a corneal scar will result in a permanent visual defect in many instances. Although sensitivity to pontocaine and fluorescein may occur, the risk of corneal damage is higher, and the procedure in almost all instances is harmless, though it should *not* be done by untrained personnel.

A team physician, a single individual who may extend his interest in athletics into the call and maintenance of his team, will be at least a valuable asset to an athletic program. He will relieve the coaching staff of the necessity of making decisions, which they really should not have to make, and by his advice will contribute to continued smooth operation of a season's work. Protection of the athlete's health will become a shared responsibility, and many permanently disabling conditions may be circumvented. Advances in medical treatment, which accrue rapidly, will be available to the athlete, for the enhancement of the entire program, and the athletic success of alma mater.

INDEX